WRESTLING
WITH
THE CHURCH

WRESTLING
WITH
THE CHURCH

One Woman's

Experience

by

MARY LEVISON

BOOK PUBLISHERS

© Mary Levison

World rights reserved by the publishers

Arthur James Limited
One Cranbourne Road
London N10 2BT
Great Britain

First published 1992

British Library Cataloguing in Publication Data
Levison, Mary
Wrestling with the Church
I: Title
274.1

ISBN 0-85305-307-3

Cover design by
The Creative House, Saffron Walden, Essex

Typeset by
John Dekker, London N20 0QG

Printed by
The Guernsey Press Co Ltd, Guernsey, Channel Islands

Acknowledgements

I am very grateful to Bishop Patrick Rodger for his generous Foreword.

I also thank the Rev James Weatherhead for reading the manuscript to ensure that I have not tarnished too badly the good name of the Church of Scotland.

Mrs Mary Millican, Miss Kay Ramsay, Deaconess, and the Rev Margaret Forrester have encouraged me to think that I have not misrepresented the story.

But none of these bears responsibility for what is here written, that responsibility being mine alone.

CONTENTS

Foreword

Foreword

One of the unfortunate effects of our Christian divisions is that churches (both large and small) are apt to pursue their internal debates as if they alone existed. Enterprising individuals may make it their business to discover how other churches in other countries have been handling the same matters but, on the whole, assemblies and synods have taken little notice of these foreign experiences, unless perhaps to use some of them as blunt instruments — i.e. largely on hearsay — on one or other side of the argument.

A good illustration of this truth is provided by the processes, often controversial, concerning the admission of women to the Orders of the Church. In particular, not much attention was paid outside Scotland to the remarkable fact that in only five years — from 1963, when Mary Levison (or Lusk as she then was) first presented her petition to the General Assembly of the Church of Scotland, to 1968 when the Assembly accepted the principle of the ordination of women to the ministry of Word and Sacraments — a great national church had been persuaded to change its mind. It was not that this church was less conservative or less male-dominated than most of its coevals; but in the first spokesman (Mary Levison would not insist on 'spokeswoman') and would-be candidate, it had someone of rare quality, skilful and articulate, patient and persistent, the author of this book.

Mary Lusk came to present her petition as a mature servant of the Church, with a notable heritage and an excellent theological training. But these were not all. She had, above all, a simple and firm conviction about her calling which refused to be browbeaten or side-tracked. She rode straight at her fences, and it is the same fearless and candid spirit which animates her telling of the story. It is a story saved from egotism by her devotion to the Church of her birth and baptism, and from triumphalism by the knowledge that the ministers and deaconesses of her sex still have some distance to go before they have fully taken their place in an institution run on masculine lines. Meanwhile, however, it is remarkable how many of the aforementioned fences have fallen within the space of thirty-odd years — fences which once looked so formidable and in many cases turned out to be so flimsy, when prejudice encountered theology.

I write this foreword as an Anglican, i.e. a member of a church which has not yet committed itself to the ordination of women to the priesthood and has agonised over the question a good deal longer than its Presbyterian neighbour. I am aware that some of my fellow-Anglicans will be inclined to dismiss the outcome in the Church of Scotland on the grounds that its theology of ministry is different in important respects from our own. Yet a reference to the Ordinal and other formularies of the Church of England might check too hasty a judgement in the matter. Just as we can discover many similarities in the arguments and hesitations which the book describes, so we can find many points in common in the exercise of the ministry of Word and Sacraments to which Mary Levison, née Lusk was, after much vigorous wrestling with the Church, admitted. It is a story to ponder and to enjoy.

† Patrick Rodger

I — God Calls

"I will not let you go unless you bless me" cried Jacob, as he wrestled with the Unknown at the brook Jabbok (Genesis 32:26). He was held inexorably in the grip of this Being who had the power to bless or to withhold blessing. He knew that he could not cross the Jordan into the land of his fathers without the blessing and the naming, the new calling to be Israel. So he wrestles and prays, and in the end is blessed and sent forth.

I have sometimes felt rather like that. My life has been lived in the grip of the Church, from which I have not felt able to free myself — either by giving it all up or by going elsewhere. I have therefore stayed and wrestled and prayed and wept, until the Church of my fathers and mothers has given me her blessing, accepted my calling and sent me forth.

You would only know yourself to be inescapably held by the Church, however, if you believed that the Church was something special. The Church is not God, as the unknown wrestler at Jabbok turned out to be. But the Church is the Body of Christ; she is the company of the baptised; she is the channel of life, the steward of the mystery of God. So there *is* no escape, even though the Church at any particular time or place may be obtuse, legalistic, slow; sometimes inhospitable and hurtful; often seeming to care more for tradition than for signs of the Holy Spirit. That is none the less where I belong — and I have to be myself and fulfil my calling within this Church. If the Church is the guardian of the great mystery which is God, then it is within the Church that I must be able to explore through to the truth which will set me free. If the Church is the channel of life, then it must be here that a woman can be freely herself in the service of the Church, just as a man can be.

The setting is then inevitably the Church, but the central character in the drama is God. What an incredibly audacious

1

claim to make! And yet none of this would have been written if I had not believed it to be true. What I have tried to write is the story of God's action in and through His Church in terms of the forms of ministry in which I have been involved — the diaconate and the Ministry of Word and Sacraments. I do believe that the Holy Spirit has been at work in my church, the Church of Scotland, over these last decades, opening up channels of ministry that were hitherto blocked; doing something to restore to the Church the wholeness and health without which the gospel loses all credibility.

I also believe that the Holy Spirit works through people, both individually and corporately. For that reason it is not possible to write of change in the Church without regard to the story of the men and women through whom change has been brought about. Theologically, persons have priority over principles. God became incarnate in a Person who declared "I am the Truth". Therefore the action of the Spirit in the lives of women and men is the stuff of Church history, of which Courts and Committees have to take account in their deliberations. For this reason I have to crave the indulgence of my readers if I write of myself as a participant in the drama.

If, however, I claim that this is the story of God's action in His Church, then I have to speak of God first and tell my own story second. I have to attempt to say something of the God in whom I believe before I go on to narrate the changes that have been brought about in ministries and what it was like to be a woman struggling in the grip of His Church.

* * * * *

"If we are led by the mysterious God, our lives will be anchored in only one certainty, that we are mysteriously called beyond ourselves" (Gerard Hughes, *In Search of a Way*, p90, Darton Longman & Todd, 1986). I only discovered the writings of the Jesuit Gerard Hughes, comparatively far on in my journey, but they cast a light backwards over my experience. The calling of which he spoke had always been for me mysterious and yet compelling. More fundamentally, "the mysterious God" of whom he wrote was the God who in Christ had drawn me: He is "the God of surprises" (to quote Hughes again), constant in His love and yet constantly doing some new thing. As a result, human living is not so much a resting in a known and static God, but an exploration and an adventure out into the unknown, relying not on what has always been but on some sort of a vision of what might be.

In 1982 New College Union (the association of former divinity students in the Faculty of Divinity at Edinburgh University) did me the honour of electing me President for the year. In October I gave my Presidential Address. I took the opportunity to try to express in words the faith by which I live, the faith which both involved me in my wrestling and carried me through it. Perhaps this personal credo, or that part of it which may explain my motivation, should be my starting-point. It was then nearly thirty years since I had graduated at Edinburgh University, having been taught by a marvellous galaxy of teachers and having absorbed biblical scholarship and systematic theology to the best of my ability. What I found myself saying thirty years later was that I believed that the more one's confidence in the central tenets of the faith grows, the more free one is to be open-minded on many questions. The more one grows in the faith, the less dogmatic one becomes. This means also that the more firmly the Church stands on the fundamentals of her own faith, the more freedom will she have, under God, to be open to the questions and challenges which are being put to her.

When faced with a calling or a challenge or the demand for change, I do not believe that either we individually or the Church corporately can retreat behind the dogmatism that finds answers in Scripture to all the minutiae of the faith or of the ordering of the Church. That is to fail to understand the centrality of Christ which means that there is a higher reference point than the words of the Bible, namely the living Christ Himself. Nor does such dogmatism leave room for the Holy Spirit who leads us into new truth, truth which is always concerning the things of Christ, but which may need to be newly formulated. It must be possible for the Church to do new things in response to the leading of the Holy Spirit.

This is not to belittle the role of Scripture or of right doctrine. I am indebted again to Gerard Hughes for the insight that "the justification of Christian doctrines and definitions is that they can help to keep the mystery open. Christian doctrine does not claim to give us adequate descriptions of God or of His Church (though it is often mistakenly thought to do so). Doctrine is offered to help us keep on the track of mystery, to help us to continue searching. Heretical doctrine is teaching which leads us down a *cul-de-sac*, diverting us from the path which leads into mystery" *(op cit)*. This humility of mind in face of the God of heaven and earth, who is also the God of the Church, is where I would hope to take my stance.

The function of the Church, as I tried to express it in my New College Union address, is "to point men and women towards a saving knowledge of God in Christ by confessing not absolute knowledge but a firm faith in the Cross and Resurrection and by admitting that beyond that much is unknown, and indeed unknowable on this side of death. Men and women are helped to live more truly and freely by being pointed not to what they can know and control but towards the ultimate mystery. If someone will let himself be called forth into the unknown by the call of Love, then he takes his first faltering steps forward into his true humanity".

Since the concept of calling is central to my "wrestling with the Church", especially in the period covered by chapters V and VI, may I also quote here some of what I said in 1982 on the calling of a Christian:

"... Our calling is a calling out into the unknown, as it was for the incarnate Jesus. He knew that He was called and claimed by love. That was the meaning of the voice heard at His baptism: 'I love you, you are mine'. But I venture to suggest that that was all of which He could be sure; any further surety or security was denied to Him — or rather He himself rejected the way of security when He faced and rejected the temptation to call on the angels to hold Him up and keep Him safe. He sought no security, except to know that He was loved and claimed by the living Spirit of God; all the rest was a colossal gamble.

"So it is also for us. Our calling is not into a great system, a vast framework of statements and creeds and standards within which we may feel secure. The Church is not a bandwagon of certainty on which we may be carried along in company with those who are sure of their salvation. We are offered only the word of life, the word that sets us free, God's word: 'You are mine, I love you'."

This is, in a sense, a plea to the Church to be open to the Spirit of God blowing through her; to exercise the spiritual freedom which she claims to possess; to venture on to unknown and untried paths; to leave the issue in God's hands.

When I addressed New College Union I did so as the first daughter to follow her father in the office of President. My father had been President in 1953, so in 1982 I said "Some of you will remember him; he was a saint and a scholar. I owe to him more than I can say, and I should be glad, if I thought it at all worthy, to dedicate this address to his memory".

5

My next task is to tell of him and my mother and family, and the roots from which I have sprung. Readers more interested in the ecclesiastical than the personal story should feel free to move on to later chapters.

II — Origins and Influences

I was born in Oxford in 1923, fourth of the family of five of David Colville Lusk and Mary Theodora (née Colville). My parents were second cousins. I never knew either of my grandfathers. My father's father, who died in 1913, was John Lusk, a baker in Coatbridge (then in Lanarkshire), where he met and married Jessie Colville, the eldest of the large family of David Colville, the steelmaker who later established his works in Motherwell. John Lusk retired early and they moved to Edinburgh, and later to Strathaven. They belonged to the United Presbyterian Church.

My grandfather was, from all accounts, a reserved, upright, religious man, full of good works. His legacy to my childhood, so far as I am aware of it, was perhaps most clearly seen in total abstinence and sabbatarianism (in which he would be no different from many of his generation), and among my hymnbooks I still have his well-used copy of *Sacred Songs and Solos* (Moody and Sankey) dated 1880.

My paternal grandmother was gentle and beautiful: she was asked by the artist Sir Joseph Noel Paton to sit for a painting of the Madonna, but declined. I remember her only in her old age when she was confined to bed after a stroke and could not speak, and I had to stand on a stool beside her bed and kiss her — a somewhat frightening experience for a small girl. She died in 1929.

John and Jessie Lusk had three children, of whom the second was my father, David, born at Broomhouse in 1881. After attending the High School of Glasgow and spending one year at the University there, he went as an undergraduate to Oxford, which is how our family's long connection with Oxford began. He read History at Balliol, where he made a number of life-long friends. One was William Temple, who later became Archbishop of Canterbury. (When Temple was made a bishop, he stood in

7

front of our fireplace, spread his hands over his somewhat expansive front and said, "Well, David, here you see before you the Abomination of Desolation!".) Returning to Edinburgh and the parental home, David went to New College, at that time the United Free Church College, where he studied for the ministry, interrupting his studies for eighteen months to go to India to teach history in Madras Christian College, and completing the course in 1909. Meantime he had become engaged in 1907 to his cousin Dora Colville, who lived with her widowed mother just along Edinburgh's Colinton Road from the Lusk home.

Dora, my mother, was the daughter of John Colville of Campbeltown. He was born in 1827, ninety-seven years before his youngest grandchild. Brought up in a pious home, he was 'converted' at the age of 17 and gave his life to Christ; then having graduated Master of Arts in Glasgow, he studied theology at the United Presbyterian Divinity Hall, attending also the Free Church College (New College) in Edinburgh. He was, however, never ordained, evidently feeling that his calling was rather what might be termed a freelance evangelist, both in his native Campbeltown and in an astonishing series of 'missions', spanning at least twenty-seven years and a huge geographical area from Orkney to Kent, but mainly all over central Scotland. On one such journey, he met Mary Agnes Bodington; they were married in 1883, but less than three years later John Colville, who had suffered from consumption for many years, died.

Mary Agnes was English. As a young woman she worked as what we might now call a parish assistant, together with Frances Ridley Havergal, in the parish of Perry Barr, Birmingham. (The vicar was a Mr Snepp, and his curates rejoiced in the names of Mr Savage and Mr Meek!) Again on my shelf of hymnbooks — very good indicators of theological and ecclesiastical fashion — I find *Songs of Grace and Glory* edited by Charles B Snepp and presented to Mary Agnes Bodington by the editor in 1878. She was active in evangelical circles, and after her marriage delighted to accompany her husband on his evangelistic work until the birth of their daughter in 1886. During her long widowhood she lived for the most part in Edinburgh, active in many good causes such as Temperance, the YWCA and the Scottish Women's Protestant Association. In her later years she lived with us in Oxford, taking delight in her grandchildren, but to the younger of them she was very much the figure of an old lady in black with the beautiful white lace 'widow's cap' which she had worn for over forty years. She died at the age of 89 in 1933 when I was ten.

Their daughter Mary Theodora, always called Dora, was thus brought up entirely by her mother. She was educated at private schools and then at the University of Edinburgh where she graduated in 1909 with an Honours Degree in Philosophy — somewhat unusual for a woman in the first decade of this century. She won the Bronze Medal for Moral Philosophy in her Intermediate Honours year. Having taken 'time-out' to travel with her mother to India to visit her fiancé in Madras, she came back to do her Honours year and obtained a 'good Second', though she had letters from both her professors — James Seth and A S Pringle-Pattison — expressing regret that she had missed her expected First. Professor Pringle-Pattison added "We shall always remember you as one of the best of the select band of ladies who have pursued philosophy to the Honours stage". Dora Colville was also active in student affairs, being President of both the Women's Debating Society and the Women's Christian Union.

My parents were married in Edinburgh in 1909, and two years later my father was ordained and inducted to the United Free Church at Innellan on the Clyde where my brother John was born. Then in 1914 he was appointed Chaplain to the Presbyterian members of the University of Oxford, an appointment made jointly by the Church of Scotland and the United Free Church of Scotland. His ministry there was interrupted by war service as a Chaplain with the London Scottish in France, where he won the MC and bar as well as the affection and admiration of the troops. Returning in 1919 he settled in Oxford until 1933. During the Oxford years David, Andrew, myself and Janet were born.

This spell of nineteen years he would probably have regarded as the major achievement of his ministry. In his time St Columba's was built, and a congregation of the Presbyterian Church of England established in 1929. But for the whole period his work was among Presbyterian members of the University, both dons and undergraduates, mainly from Scotland but a good number from overseas, wherever the Reformed faith was professed. Among the senior members who worshipped in St Columba's were such eminent scholars as A D Lindsay, W D Ross, F M Powicke, M N Tod, and A S Russell. I remember all of these reading Scripture regularly at morning service, while my earliest recollection of a Communion Service is of John Buchan standing with a cup, serving the wine. My father's leading of worship and preaching was always scholarly and lucid, and greatly appreciated by both 'town and gown'. In every term there would be a visit from some eminent preacher from North of the Border — George MacLeod, Charles Warr and Harry Miller, for example.

Being himself a Balliol man, my father was able to enter into the life of that curious animal which is Oxford University, and he loved it. Whether cycling along the towpath coaching one of the Balliol boats, picnicking with the family in Eights Week, dining at High Table or joining in discussions on history or theology, he was at his ease. We lived in a large house in South Parks Road with a domestic staff which today would be unthinkable in a manse. Every Sunday was open house at tea-time, and four days a week undergraduates came to lunch in twos and threes. Sixty years later I still frequently meet people who speak appreciatively of my parents' hospitality, by which they mean not only meals, but also caring concern and interesting conversation. My mother, of course, was in her element in that role, as well as in leading Bible Study groups for women undergraduates.

Such was my childhood home. We were a large family, sometimes of three generations when my grandmother Colville lived with us, and with an almost continuously open house in term-time. Coming in to lunch from school, we took our places at a huge table and could find ourselves beside a Scot — anyone from a peer's son to a Trade Union sponsored undergraduate from Ruskin College — or an Indian or American or South African; and the talk was away over our heads. But it was a marvellously happy home, and we all enjoyed our first schools — the Dragon School for the boys and the Oxford High School for Girls for Janet and me. John went on to Winchester and David to Rugby. By 1933, my parents had decided that they did not want the family to grow up entirely anglicised, and that it was time to move back to Scotland, if there should be an opportunity. More than that, it would probably be right to make way for a younger man. A call was offered to my father from West Coates Church, Edinburgh, and in the summer of 1933 we all moved North.

Scotland was not unknown to us because every summer we spent six weeks or so at Machrihanish near Campbeltown in Argyll. This involved a huge trek north in 'Belinda', a seven-seater touring Buick, supplemented by train and boat for the overflow. It took us three days by road with sometimes a stopover in Edinburgh to visit grandmothers. Machrihanish was another world — sand and sea, golf-course and farmyard, expeditions of all sorts and lots of people — friends and relations staying with us, other families who were regular visitors like ourselves and many memorable local characters. My family had a house there all my childhood years, so there is a sense in which our Scottish roots were in Argyll throughout the Oxford period.

But Edinburgh was something else, and was somewhat of a culture shock to me at the age of ten. Oxford seemed to be an integrated community: the most outwardly disreputable were probably the most eminent! But in Edinburgh life was polarised. In Sunday School (which was itself a new experience) the children of the tenements of Haymarket and Dalry were different from the Oxford children: and on weekdays, Janet and I were at St Monica's, a private school, with the daughters of lawyers and judges and the New Town élite. I did not feel at home with either, and was unhappy at first. But in retrospect I have often been grateful that I was faced with this adjustment at an early age, and was able to watch my parents' ease in all company and gradually come to feel at home myself with everyone. West Coates was an important counterbalance to St Monica's: an Oxford accent was more likely to be modified there.

The reason my parents sent us to St Monica's was that this would give us a chance to do the entrance examination for St Leonard's School in St Andrews to which they planned we should go at the age of 13 — which we duly did. There I enjoyed five years of education, sport and friendships; we were fortunate to have a marvellously cultured and companionable housemistress; and Church meant usually Hope Park until some of us hived off to hear Donald Baillie, *locum tenens* in the vacancy at Martyrs. I then gained a place at Lady Margaret Hall, Oxford, whither I returned as an undergraduate in 1941. Both boarding-school and single-sex schools and colleges are matters for debate: I did not, of course, choose my school (though I did to some extent choose LMH), but I certainly enjoyed it and am very aware how fortunate I was.

Oxford, even in wartime, was a good experience. I chose to read Philosophy, Politics and Economics, switching from languages to which school seemed to be leading. We worked hard, and in our spare time had to "dig for victory" and firewatch at nights; but there was time also for societies of all sorts and singing in the Bach Choir, for sport and punting on the river. And there was, of course, St Columba's, a home from home for me; I was confirmed by the Rev Ian Miller in the same church where eighteen years earlier I had been baptised by the Anglican Chaplain of Balliol.

Meantime, as a family, we were being hit pretty hard. My mother died in 1938 at the age of 52. Since returning to Scotland she had taken up again some of her previous interests and was active in the Women's Foreign Mission, Women's Home Mission and on the Board of St Colm's College, as well as in West Coates. In fact she seemed to me to be for ever 'going to meetings' to an extent which I was on the verge of resenting. But she, nevertheless, was the hub of the family, and was a great letter-writer when we were all away from home. Her death, after months of poor health, left a huge gap.

I think we had always been aware that our mother was different from some of our friends' mothers, particularly in Edinburgh, in that she was more academic, and that, for her, spiritual matters were of greater moment than clothes, food and drink, and other material things, although she was always concerned to have an attractive home and she liked to dress well. I have only two of her writings, but they are typical of her loves and interests: the first is a fascinating eye-witness account of the 'Edinburgh 1910' World Missionary Conference with a critique of the issues raised by that great gathering. The second is a rendering into English of the Latin lines of the carol *In dulci jubilo* so that everyone could enjoy one of her favourite hymns. Her legacy to the family was a loving, secure and open home and wide horizons of the mind and spirit.

In 1940 David was killed. A brilliant, likeable, amusing brother, training as a Chartered Acountant to work in Colvilles Steel, he had followed his father and John to Balliol where he was in the Oxford University Air Squadron. Called up with the RAF Volunteer Reserve at the beginning of the war, he was posted missing after a Coastal Command bombing raid and is buried in Holland.

In 1942 came another dreaded telegram, this time from the War Office to say that Andrew was "missing" in the Western Desert. He had only had one year at Hertford College, Oxford, after Rugby School and then went with the King's Own Royal Regiment to India, Iraq and Egypt. At the age of 21, he tried to stop a tank advancing by leaping on to the running-board and was shot dead. Andrew was less intellectually inclined than his brothers, but he had so many other gifts and interests — friendliness and a great sense of humour, a love of animals and the countryside, and great courage.

What an incredible waste of life! What a yawning void in our family! And what a sense of responsibility for those of us who were left. John was by now serving in the Royal Air Force as a chaplain, Janet in the Auxiliary Territorial Service so when, in 1943, I was called up after a shortened course at Oxford, I had the option of the Civil Service, which could mean St Andrew's House in Edinburgh and therefore living at home with my father. This I thought was the right thing to do, though it was by now a somewhat desolate home. I spent three years as a Temporary Administrative Assistant in the Scottish Home Department, enjoying my work, learning about administration, and leaving with a great respect for the integrity and hard work of senior civil servants.

After the war was over there was a chance to return to Oxford to turn the shortened degree into a full one, so I went back for four terms, specialising in philosophy and greatly enjoying the life of a post-war student.

But at the end of that, and with a First Class degree, what should I do? The Appointments Board suggested a typing-course; the Civil Service turned me down at the Selection

14

School for a permanent appointment; I was really very undecided and for a time went home to live again with my father. However, this meant time on my hands, which turned out to mean time to get more and more involved with the Girls' Association, a Church of Scotland organisation for girls and young women.

III — The Girls' Association

The Girls' Association is now (1992) virtually unknown in the Church of Scotland and remembered only by those of a certain age. It went out of existence in 1954 and its members were aged 15-30. Those who remember it well and whose lives were influenced by it are now in their sixties or more.

Nonetheless, the GA is, I think, well worth recalling because in the first half of this century it was large and influential and has, in fact, never been replaced. It never will be: it belonged to its time, and times have changed. But there are many of us who would not have done what we have done, nor be what we are today, had it not been for the GA. It certainly played a decisive role in directing me along the way I have travelled.

"You won't believe this," a lady said to me a few months ago at a Woman's Guild meeting in Ayrshire, "it's a long time ago now, but it was only in the GA that I came to understand what the gospel was all about. I went to Church and Sunday School, and it seemed to be all 'Do's and Don'ts' and being good, but when I went to GA Bible Schools and heard people like John and Donald Baillie, I realised that the gospel was about grace and forgiveness."

I believed her all right: your average run-of-the-mill children's sermon has a lot to answer for. The GA opened doors and widened horizons and sounded new depths for two generations of young women in the Scottish churches. It gave us a fuller understanding of the faith and an appreciation of what it means to belong to the One Holy Catholic Church in all the world. It did for the whole membership of the Church (provided they were young and female) what the SCM did for those fortunate enough to be students.

In origin the GA owed its existence to the fact that, at the turn of the century, there were girls at the Universities who had not only Christian commitment but also vision and great ability. Some of them were involved in the Student Volunteer Movement, offering for missionary service overseas under the banner "The Evangelisation of the World in this Generation". They were very go-ahead girls and, when two of them found that at an Edinburgh meeting of the Women's Missionary Association of the United Free Church they were the only two who were under the age of thirty, they asked themselves why missions should have become the province of old ladies. Why did the Church not give opportunities to young people rather than expect them to help in organisations run by their elders?

It was on the initiative of these two girls — Eleanor Lorimer and Bessie Smart — that there came into being in 1901 the Girls' Auxiliary to the Women's Missionary Association. It quickly took root and grew because it was in tune with the missionary enthusiasm of the time. As its name suggests, its initial aim was to be auxiliary to the Women's Missionary Association, that is to say to harness the gifts and enthusiasm of the under-30s in support of the great overseas mission of the United Free Church of Scotland. Over the years its aims may have deepened and widened, but that first focus on mission was never lost. When, eighteen years later, the Girls' Guild was formed in the Church of Scotland, the emphasis was more on social service within Scotland and, when the two came together at the Union of the Churches in 1929, the interests of those two groups merged and the re-united Church benefited from an organisation of 20,000 members, committed to worship, study, giving and service to a very impressive degree. The united body was called the Girls' Association.

The most distinctive achievement of the GA was the support of our own missionaries, both financially and personally through correspondence and intercessory prayer. Starting in 1905 with one 'sixpenny missionary' (each member to give a sixpence), and increasing over the years to ten (of whom eight were overseas and two in Scotland), the

GA membership was entirely responsible for meeting their salaries. They were appointed by the Women's Foreign Mission, the Women's Home Mission and the Ladies' Highland Association, so that they were in the fullest sense servants of the whole Church. But their selection as Girls' Own Missionaries (how quaint that title sounds today!) was in the hands of the GA and many were themselves GA or ex-GA members. This kindled a lively interest in the world-wide Church, and a recognition that we were all involved in service in many lands through our own chosen representatives. As Professor John Foster of Glasgow University commented in a radio broadcast about the GA, "It is organisations like these that *grow* most of the women who offer themselves as missionaries". The money required for their support was mostly from personal contributions, willingly given since the missionaries were known personally to many in the GA through furlough visits to Conferences, Bible Schools, Branch meetings and so on.

Study of the World Church had then a prominent place in the activities of GA branches, most of which met once a week on a weekday evening. Also important were study of the faith, and Bible Study, in which various methods were pioneered. Worship was led by the members themselves and it is remarkable how many GA groups held Weekend Retreats long before retreats became common.

If all that sounds unbearably earnest and onerous, nothing could be further from the truth. There was always about the GA an air of gaiety and laughter which rightly belongs with the real mission of the Church; and good friendships, many of them lifelong, were formed. The key to it was perhaps that the whole movement was entirely self-governing: this was a pioneering youth organisation which threw up its own leadership and managed its own affairs not only in branches but at presbyterial and national levels as well. With elected office-bearers and a salaried staff at headquarters, the GA produced literature and organised Bible Schools —

memorable weekends with many very distinguished speakers, often at Bonskeid, the YMCA Conference Centre near Pitlochry in Perthshire — Retreats and Training Courses, and an annual Conference which filled the Church's Assembly Hall in Edinburgh or Wellington Church in Glasgow. The GA was therefore a marvellous training-ground for many of us: it was there that we learned such skills as we may have in public speaking, chairing meetings and organising events.

The Second World War was, of course, difficult for any youth organisation and membership inevitably declined, though the missionary commitment was maintained. After the war, times had changed: single-sex organisations no longer attracted, and Youth Fellowships came on to the scene. These Sunday evening gatherings did not have the same outlook nor did they carry the same responsibility as the GA, but they did face us with a problem. Girls could hardly be expected to belong to both (though some did) and, as the mixed Fellowships increased, the GA decreased. 10,000 in 1945 became 7,000 in 1949 and 3,000 in 1953, with an inevitable reduction in missionary support.

In 1951 the Jubilee of the GA was celebrated with a great sense of praise and gratitude. Much of the old spirit of enthusiasm was recaptured and, true to the original aims, money was given to sponsor three Jubilee Bursars from the Younger Churches at St Colm's College for a year. But after that, hard decisions had to be taken. The question was whether to hold on until the organisation finally faded out, or to recognise that the GA had made its contribution in those fifty years and should now disband, encouraging its members to put their strength into the Youth Fellowship movement. We chose the latter course, and the GA dissolved itself in 1954.

The history of the GA was written in 1950 by Kay Young, a prominent educationalist and herself an ex-President. In her final assessment of the part which the GA had played in

19

the Church she wrote: "The GA has always had the vision of the One Holy Catholic Church, and of the mighty plan of God being worked out in the world. It has always possessed the spirit of youth and adventure, and has dedicated that spirit to the Master 'Whose we are and Whom we serve'. It has always believed that God will accept the gift of the life of each individual and that each of us has her own particular part in the great plan of God. It has always asked God to enable it by thought, prayer and service to prepare for greater responsibility in the furtherance of His Kingdom. These are the great eternal things, the things that do not grow old or out-of-date" (*Our Sail We Lift*, Girls' Association, 1950, pp78-79).

That is as good a tribute as we could want. Such an organisation might today be considered old-fashioned, pious, too church-centred, but it trained and shaped many of us; and by this legacy I believe the GA made an important contribution to the ongoing process of the opening up of new avenues of service for women in the Church of Scotland throughout the twentieth century.

*   *   *   *   *

I joined the GA in 1946 in my father's congregation of West Coates, but it was not until the following year, on my return from Oxford, that I was able to be an active member on a wider front. I was then asked to become Editor of the quarterly magazine *The Trailmaker*: with the kind and helpful encouragement of Dr J W Stevenson, the then Editor of *Life and Work* (the official magazine of the Church of Scotland), I made my first modest ventures into writing and editing. But in 1948 I handed the magazine over to my successor on my election as Central President. This appointment was for two years and so from 1948 to 1950 I had the great privilege of moving about Scotland visiting and speaking at branches, taking part in weekend activities of all sorts, chairing committees, Bible Schools and the big Central Conference, and all the time making friends from all over the country. It was a time of great opportunity for me, one which I hope I used to the full. When it came to the Jubilee in 1951 I was asked to chair the planning committee and then the Jubilee Conference in the Assembly Hall in Edinburgh, a memorable experience.

As Central President of the GA I also found myself chairing a Young People's Holiday Conference at a camp near Edinburgh, as well as a large Assembly Hall Rally organised by the Foreign Mission Committee entitled "World Church Calling Youth". And when the Assembly's Youth Committee proposed that the young people of the Church should get together to consider and face the Challenge of Communism, I was on the steering committee of the First Christian Youth Assembly in which the GA played its part alongside other young people's organisations from all the churches in Scotland.

As President I represented the GA on the Women's Foreign Mission and Women's Home Mission Committees, so I found myself at the very places where the Church's need for women to serve abroad and at home was discussed and made known. I could not help but be aware that missionaries and deaconesses were needed, and I began to wonder whether that included me.

These were the two avenues of service which the Church offered to women in the 1940s. I think it has to be said that though young women graduates might find plenty of scope in the service of the Church overseas — as doctors and surgeons, as college lecturers and teachers, as nurses and in other professional capacities — most of my contemporaries, looking at how the Church would use them at home, turned instead to one of the other caring professions. I have often reflected that at that time the Church lost to the social work profession many able young women who could not see a career for themselves in the Church. It was, of course, immensely important that many women with a Christian commitment entered social work and were able to bring their insights and values to bear on their work of caring. But if there are also to be people professionally dedicated to building up the Body of Christ, then it must be said that the Church has been very slow to use women to their full potential within its own life.

For myself, I was not any more dedicated than the others. But I had had, as I have already explained, quite exceptional opportunities to hear of the Church's needs through the GA, so perhaps that was the direction for me. To go overseas for a lifetime — which was at that time what was meant by 'foreign mission' service — did not seem fair for family reasons. So what about being a deaconess? What about putting on the grey suit and hat, which constituted the deaconess uniform, and working in a parish as an employee of the Women's Home Mission Committee and being for always No. 2 in the team? A few years earlier it would have been a matter of being a 'Church Sister', but since 1949 all were called Deaconess. That was at least a biblical title; but deaconesses were in an 'Order', and what about being a member of an Order? And what of spending two years at St Colm's College: how would that follow on after Oxford?

Of course there is a sense in which none of these difficulties should weigh if one is called to serve, yet I do not believe that God calls people through frustration and denial of gifts. He calls rather through a realisation that one might be able to make a contribution by the offering of all that one is and has been given. He calls also through the Church's willingness to open up opportunities; and here there was a chink of light appearing under the door. In 1949 the General Assembly of the Church of Scotland approved a Revised Scheme for the Order of Deaconesses which said that some deaconesses might have a full theological training, equivalent to that required for the ministry and with such a training behind them they might be licensed to conduct public worship and to preach. Maybe that was for me: maybe I was wanted. So I offered to the Women's Home Mission, the employing committee of deaconesses.

I well remember that one of the interviewing panel was Miss Marjorie Moinet, a friend of my mother from forty years before, and she said "Go and get as full a training as is available to you, and that means — as well as a time at St Colm's — taking the Bachelor of Divinity course at New College". The Committee agreed that I should do this as a candidate for the Order of Deaconesses, with a view to becoming a "Deaconess licensed to preach".

Women at New College (the Faculty of Divinity of Edinburgh University) were not very common. There was one other in my year and one in the year before me; the former went into Religious Education and the latter into the ministry of the United Free Church, by then open to women. We were not, of course, candidates for the ministry of the Church of Scotland and so were not 'regular students' — the chief consequence of which was that we did not have to do the Bible Examination. On the other hand, we received no book grant and had to pay more for our lunch. The three-year BD course comprised Old Testament, New Testament, Church History and Systematic Theology, with an option to specialise in one of those subjects. I chose Systematic Theology. I also took the full Practical Theology course on the assumption that it might be important for work as an assistant in a parish and for licensing as a preacher to have taken courses on Christian ethics, homiletics, Church law and so on.

There was also a requirement for deaconess candidates to have "a period of residence and attendance at some classes" at St Colm's College, the Church's own training college for missionaries, deaconesses and youth workers. So in my second year at New College I lived at St Colm's (where Dr Olive Wyon was Principal), sharing in corporate worship and Bible Study and doing practical training in congregations under the direction of St Colm's staff. In that way I had the best of both worlds; and I have always been grateful to have participated in these two very different and normally quite separate forms of training which the Church has considered appropriate for ministers on the one hand and deaconesses on the other. The former was almost entirely academic, the latter much less so and with greater emphasis on worship and the devotional life, on practical training, on community and group or team work.

My professors at New College represented a wealth of scholarship. Norman Porteous and Oliver Rankin in Old Testament; William Manson and James Stewart in New Testament; J H S Burleigh in Church History; and in Theology, John Baillie and Tom Torrance with their very different approaches. After Oxford I found the teaching and examination systems strange, but soon adapted and greatly enjoyed my three years, making good friends and being entirely accepted, I think, by my colleagues once they realised that a woman could actually be a perfectly respectable theologian. In the end of the day I was awarded a Distinction in Systematic Theology and the Aitken Fellowship.

I was, in fact, firmly intending — at the age of 30 — to go straight into a parish as a deaconess, but was persuaded that this Fellowship (which was not limited to candidates for the ministry) would enable me to gain wider experience by living and studying abroad. The mecca for students of Reformed theology in those days was Basel in Switzerland, where the great Karl Barth was teaching. The suggestion was, however, that I should spend the winter semester in Heidelberg and the following summer semester in Basel. Professor Edmund Schlink, an eminent Lutheran theologian, received an honorary doctorate in Divinity from Edinburgh the year that I graduated BD (1953) and, at the suggestion of Professor Torrance, Professor Schlink stayed in our home which gave me an introduction to this charming, open-minded and ecumenical theologian, soon to be elected Rektor of the University of Heidelberg. A certain post-war reluctance to go to Germany was mitigated by this and by the fact that, in a time of acute housing shortage, I was able to get a room in the house of Frau von Kuenssberg, mother of a family who had been friends of our family before the war and who was herself President of the University Women in Heidelberg, who held meetings in my room. There were not yet many British students in Heidelberg — I recall none in the faculty of theology — but I found a good welcome in the Studentengemeinde (SCM).

I looked on these months in Germany as an opportunity to get to know the German Church and also the deaconess scene, so different from our own. The first of my many visits to Deaconess Motherhouses was to Grossheppach, near Stuttgart, where I spent Christmas. I shall write later of the German Motherhouse Diaconate with its roots at Kaiserswerth on the Rhine in the middle years of the 19th century. Meantime I simply note that my acquaintance with these dedicated, hospitable Sisters goes back to my student days; and that this experience was as important for what lay ahead as the more formal lectures and seminars at Heidelberg and the friendship of the Schlinks and other academic families to whom I had introductions.

I then went on to Basel where I lived in the Baslermissionhaus (the first and only woman resident), where I found the worship of the Reformed Church very arid and where I struggled to understand the Swiss accent of Professor Karl Barth as he read to his class the next instalment of his *Kirchliche Dogmatik* which, in the summer semester of 1954, happened to be "die Sünde als Dummheit" (Sin as Folly). But Barth was also holding a seminar on "Christ, the Hope of the World", the theme of the Second Assembly of the World Council of Churches which was to be held at Evanston in the United States that summer. That I also attended because I had just been invited to go to Evanston as the youth representative from the Church of Scotland.

★　★　★　★　★

Ecumenical and international conferences of churches, involving travel and expenses which have ultimately to come from the weekly offerings of members, are regarded by some with a certain scepticism. Can the expense really be justified in terms of the return to the participating churches? What do we, the local congregations, get out of these jamborees? Why does it always seem to be the same small circle of people selected to go?

I have to plead guilty to being one of those who have had far more than their fair share of travel and ecumenical experiences at the expense of the Church. First it was a 'young person' (at 31) known to the powers-that-be through being prominent in the GA. Later it was either as a deaconess with a certain knowledge of languages (limited though that was) or as one of the then rare breed of theologically trained women (and how often have I been the 'token woman' in committees and conferences!). I think it has to be admitted, too, that once you acquire a little experience of the ecumenical world, then the Church tends to send you again — and again. All I can say in mitigation is that I have always tried to take very seriously my obligation to the constituency that sent me. That means, of course, a lot of hard work both in preparation and even more in reporting back. After Evanston, for example, there was a huge programme of follow-up meetings all over the country, and I spoke at some forty of them. The Church has to see the spin-off from international conferences in terms both of such reporting back and of changed people. For there is no doubt that such experiences have a profound effect on the participants, giving them a new or renewed sense of the One Holy Catholic Church; and the hope is that such people can then share this awareness with others.

My first international conference was in August 1949 when I was invited to join a group of young people attending a Conference of Presbyterian Youth at Montpellier in France, the first such conference organised by the World Presbyterian Alliance (now the World Alliance of Reformed Churches). As a theological student I twice attended the tripartite Anglo-Orthodox-Presbyterian Conferences organised by the Theological Colleges Department of the SCM, one on Iona and the other at Bièvres near Paris; these were memorable opportunities for sharing in Orthodox worship. Then came the invitation to Evanston and, in preparation for that, a gathering of all the European youth delegates in Berlin. Of that I chiefly remember my first meeting with East European young people, the division of the city itself and being swept up into the May Day demonstrations in East Berlin.

My trip to the USA in the summer of 1954 — out by the 'Mauretania' and back on the 'Queen Mary' — lasted for two months and included no fewer than four conferences. There was first the Assembly of the World Presbyterian Alliance at Princeton; then a youth conference before Evanston; the World Council of Churches Assembly at Evanston; and after that a Faith and Order Conference at McCormick Theological Seminary in Chicago. At all of these I was a youth delegate: we were not full participants, but we had marvellous opportunities of listening to great church leaders both in plenary sessions and in groups, and I think we all regarded these conferences as learning experiences. That might not be so today, when young people are eager to express their own views; perhaps we were all rather late developers.

In 1954 the World Council of Churches was still dominated by European and American churches; there was only the beginning of representation from the churches of Asia, Africa, Latin America, Australia and New Zealand. An example of this imbalance was the fact that of the new

Central Committee appointed at Evanston, the UK and Eire had more representatives (ten) than the whole of Africa and Latin America together (six). It is also interesting to find that of the official delegates to the Conference, 383 were clergy, 75 laymen and only 44 women. Since that time the WCC has made huge advances in becoming more truly representative of the churches worldwide and of their total membership. The accession of the Orthodox Churches has been very important in this respect.

Evanston was nevertheless an important stage on the way. This Assembly inherited the covenant made between the churches at the first Assembly in Amsterdam in 1948: "We intend to stay together" and then went on to say "To stay together is not enough. We must go forward". The Assembly called on all member churches to further the process of growing together into the unity which Christ wills for His Church. I was fascinated by the Faith and Order discussions both at Evanston and at the meeting in Chicago afterwards, because it seemed to me that the recovery of the unity of the Church was the most important function of the WCC. What form that unity should take was to be thrashed out at later Assemblies, but I am not sure that we have ever quite recaptured the enthusiasm for unity engendered by Amsterdam and Evanston. For me, however, the strongest impression left by Evanston was that of the great figures of the Church. Lilje and Niemöller of Germany; Hromadka from Czechoslovakia; D T Niles of Ceylon; Lesslie Newbigin, Bishop in South India; our own John Baillie. Guest speakers included President Eisenhower and the United Nations' Secretary-General, Dag Hammarskjöld.

With all this wisdom ringing in my ears, I left Evanston and Chicago with a good friend, Geoff Shaw (one of my year at New College and later to become Convener of Strathclyde Regional Council) for a tour of New England. When we returned to Scotland Geoff went straight into his lifelong ministry in the Gorbals, Glasgow, and I to my first deaconess appointment at Inveresk, Musselburgh, near Edinburgh.

IV — Deaconess of the Church of Scotland

Where do I now stand in relation to the Church? In 1954 I am aware that the Church employs people to do its work: if you are a man you become a minister, and if you are a woman you become a deaconess. I am in the unusual position of being trained for either, but I do not at this point question the distinction which the Church makes between men and women and I have put myself at the disposal of the Church as a candidate for the Order of Deaconesses.

I was at that time frequently asked why I did not consider the ordained ministry of the Congregational Union of Scotland or the United Free Church of Scotland where (according to the questioner) my gifts and training would have been more fully used. I did not doubt for a moment that such gifts as I had would find ample scope as a parish deaconess, as indeed proved to be the case. But, more importantly, I knew myself to be inescapably held within the Church of Scotland. We do not choose the denomination to which we will belong to suit our own convenience. The Church is not a club in which one can transfer membership to the most congenial branch. The Church of Scotland was not only the Church of my parents and of my personal roots. It was for me the manifestation of the One Holy Catholic Church in Scotland, the Church both Catholic and Reformed as described in the Declaratory Articles (*Articles Declaratory of the Constitution of the Church of Scotland in Matters Spiritual, appended to the Church of Scotland Act, 1921*). That Church had chosen me, and not I it; so there was, in fact, no option for me but the Church of Scotland.

As to the capacity in which one might serve the Church, it has always been my conviction that the Church is unduly restrictive in its conceptions of ministry. People have an immense range of gifts to offer, and the Church's task requires people who can function in a multiplicity of ways. To restrict the professional ministry of the Church to those with an academic theological training, to expect them to be all of the same mould and all to be men would seem to be wasteful of many potential offers of useful service. I can't help asking, Why? I have the kind of mind — not particularly creative or imaginative but analytical — which cannot refrain from asking questions about meaning and purpose. But obviously such questions are better asked from inside than from outside. So if the lines of ministry are to be redrawn; if, in particular, the distinction between the ordained ministry and the rest is to be no longer made on grounds of sex, then one has to plunge in to wherever the Church sees fit to put one and ask the questions from inside. While my erstwhile fellow students went on to have charge of parishes and to rule the Church through its Courts, I became an employee of a committee which appointed me to a parish as a deaconess. I was happy and fully stretched in my parish work, but almost immediately I started asking questions about what had been known in the Church of Scotland since 1888 as the Order of Deaconesses.

It is not possible within the compass of this book to give a complete history of "The Order of Deaconesses", "The Order of the Diaconate" (a phrase used as early as 1895), "Church Sisters", "The Diaconate of Women"; of the many Committees of the Established Church, the United Free Church and, since 1929, the re-united Church of Scotland charged by their Assemblies with organising, employing, caring for these women. It is a story fraught with hesitations, uncertainties and frustrations as the Church has attempted to make room for the service of women within its hitherto entirely male structures. But from the present perspective, it is interesting to look back and recall some of the milestones along the way and the principles which guided the movement. For *movement* it was, and is; there has

31

been scarcely a decade in which there has not been change and development.

There is no doubt that over the first one hundred years the Order or Office of Deaconess was conceived as an avenue of service specifically for women. Within the pre-Union Church of Scotland the initiator of the whole idea was the Rev Dr Archibald Charteris, Professor of New Testament in Edinburgh, Moderator of the General Assembly in 1892. In his capacity as Convener of the Committee on Christian Life and Work, Dr Charteris put to the Assembly in 1885 the view that the organisation of women's work in the Church was "of pressing interest". He believed that there were vast untapped resources among the women of the congregations of the Church. The question was sent to Kirk Sessions for discussion, and many of them seem to have echoed the question which was in the mind of Dr Charteris himself. "Why not revive the ancient and scriptural Order of Deaconesses?" This was an idea which he developed in his Baird Lectures of 1887 and in that same year he laid before the Assembly his scheme for the organisation of women's work, which was for the formation of a Woman's Guild to be organised in three grades: (i) the Guild, open to all women engaged in the service of Christ; (ii) a higher grade of Woman Workers in congregations; and (iii) a still higher grade of Deaconesses, trained in an Institution set up for that purpose, and set apart by the Presbytery at a religious service. This was the so-called pyramid, whose broad base was the Woman's Guild, tapering upwards through Guild leaders or women workers to the deaconesses. In the event the middle 'grade' seems not to have taken hold, but the Woman's Guild and the deaconesses were established by the Assemblies of 1887, the deaconesses to be leaders of the Guild. The first deaconess, the Lady Grisell Baillie, was 'set apart' in 1888.

From the beginning, then, there would appear to be a certain tension built into the conception of the Order of

Deaconesses: on the one hand they were to be an integral part of the women's section of the Church; on the other hand they were to be holders of an office which can be traced back to New Testament times. On the latter point Professor Charteris was very clear. On his gravestone at Wamphray in Dumfriesshire are inscribed the words: "Through his efforts the Order of Deaconesses in the Church of Scotland was restored, and the Guilds of the Church were instituted". The word "restored" is of prime importance: what was in the mind of Dr Charteris, and what the General Assembly resolved upon, was nothing less than the restoration of the scriptural office of deaconess which had been in abeyance since perhaps the 5th or 6th century AD. This, as we were to come to realise, was the absolutely right foundation on which to build: but the seeds of difficulty and confusion were sown in the not entirely compatible vision of deaconesses as leaders of 'women's work'.

The first controversy, which has actually persisted for a century, was whether deaconesses should be ordained by a Presbytery, which would be natural for those holding a scriptural office. Dr Charteris proposed that they should be so ordained. Early Christian writers, he pointed out, speak of the ordination of deaconesses "as the same with the ordination received by men". He therefore advocated that "women who are officials of the Church have a right to ordination from the Church", and ordination would be an act of the Presbytery. However, there were objections in Presbyteries on the ground, for example, that it would put the deaconess "above the elder" if she were ordained by Presbytery. To keep the peace and get the proposal through, Dr Charteris agreed to the deaconess being "set apart" by the Kirk Session — which was the situation right up to 1949, when commissioning by the Presbytery became the rule.

The next development, in 1893, also confused the issue so far as the status of women serving the Church was concerned. Because there was only a small number of deaconesses and they tended to be ladies of independent means exercising a freedom of choice as to where they would serve, the needs of the parishes were not being met. The Home Mission Committee reported that those parishes which most needed qualified women to work in depressed urban areas were least able to bear the expense of their employment. Thus was introduced the idea of the central financing and appointment of women workers to areas of need. They were called Parish Sisters and they were agents or employees of the Home Mission Committee and supported financially by the Women's Association for Home Missions, an arm of the Woman's Guild.

Thus there developed side by side two avenues of service for women: the Order of Deaconesses with a certain status but not sufficient organisation and finance to meet the needs of the Church, and the Parish Sisters who were very useful in places of need but to whom the Church gave no ecclesiastical status except as employees of a Committee and agents of a Women's Association. Again, there are seeds of future controversy here when questions come to be raised about relationships to 'employing Committees' and Church Courts.

To turn to the United Free Church, it was 1916 when their General Assembly authorised the institution of a ministry to be known as that of Church Sister. Church Sisters were trained at the Women's Missionary College (St Colm's) and were appointed by the Women's Home Mission Committee. This position was similar to that of Parish Sisters in the Church of Scotland: they were agents or employees of the Committee, 'set apart' at a service arranged by the Kirk Session.

At the Union of the Churches in 1929, the three groups were of approximately equal strength: there were in the Church of Scotland 62 Deaconesses and 53 Parish Sisters, and in the United Free Church about 60 Church Sisters.

Provision was made in the Plan of Union for a Home Department to take over the direction of all three groups; but in the event what happened was that the name Parish Sister was discontinued; Deaconesses and Church Sisters pursued separate and distinct courses until their amalgamation in 1949. It has been said that during those twenty years the Deaconesses had presented the United Church with a perpetual constitutional problem, while the Church Sisters, as employees of Committees, were no problem at all. The question was whether the 1949 Scheme which made all into deaconesses would solve all problems or provide the Church with a new set of questions. "The Order of Deaconesses as now constituted is in historic continuity with the Order of Deaconesses founded by authority of the General Assembly of the Church of Scotland in May 1887." That sounds splendid, but does the Church know what it is saying when the Assembly makes that declaration? Already in 1950, the Central Committee of the Order are throwing out questions for all deaconesses to discuss, probably new lines of thought for those who had been Church Sisters: What is the special office or function of a deaconess? What is meant by an "Order of Deaconesses"? What is the relation of the Order to the Courts and Committees of the Church?

★　★　★　★　★

As I have already mentioned, one of the provisions of the 1949 Scheme was that deaconesses with a theological training equivalent to that of ministers could serve as assistants in parishes, conducting public worship and preaching. On that basis I was appointed by the Women's Home Mission Committee in 1954 to the parish of St Michael's Inveresk at Musselburgh. My remit was to lay the foundations of a new congregation which was to be established in three housing schemes on the eastern fringe of that vast parish. The minister of Inveresk, Dr David Stiven, had two other assistants who were probationers for the ministry and who, under his supervision, ministered one at Wallyford and the other at Whitecraig and Smeaton, three outlying villages all within the parish. We were therefore a team of inexperienced workers led in a most wise, generous and imaginative way by the well-loved Dr Stiven, and fed frequently by Mrs Stiven who cheerfully added these assistants to her already large family. I was living in digs in the old village of Levenhall, part of the new parish-to-be, my chief recollection of that somewhat primitive accommodation being that there was no electricity, but gas lighting — in the 1950s!

Typical of Dr Stiven was that he was willing to treat me on exactly the same footing as his male assistants; I took my full share in preaching and leading worship in Inveresk and at Wallyford, Whitecraig and Smeaton. In my area of Pinkie Braes and Pinkiehill there was no church; in Pinkie Braes, which was furthest away from Inveresk and therefore most in need of its own ministry, there was no public building of any kind in which people could be gathered for worship. People were concerned for their children in particular, and encouraged me to make some provision for them. So I started House Sunday Schools, a network of young mothers who met once a week with me to prepare worship and teaching, and on Sunday had a group of children in their own sitting-rooms. By the time the Church Hall was built two years later, we had 170 children coming to worship in about a dozen homes. It was a lot of work in terms of training and the provision of books and equipment, but there was an enthusiasm which made it all enjoyable and which spread around the whole housing scheme. The fact that we were only scratching the surface of the need was manifest when the new Hall was opened and on the first Sunday 400 children poured in! (How to organise a picnic for that lot with no buses booked and no money? We invited the Musselburgh Pipe Band to play us along the road and the

Chief Constable to lead the way, and we had the best picnic ever in Pinkie Park.)

House groups both for Sunday worship and for Bible Study were also organised, and I did a great deal of visiting, house-to-house all round the area and in cases of need. The time came for the delineation of the new parish and the appointment of a minister to take charge. There was a certain assumption in the parish that I would be their minister, and I think they would have been quite happy if this had been possible. It was not possible, of course, and this was perhaps for me the first realisation that I was going to come up against barriers which seemed unreasonably to limit what I was permitted to do. However the minister appointed to this new Church Extension charge was the Rev Duncan Finlayson, and he and I worked happily together for a year.

One remarkable feature of the launch of the new congregation was that Dr Stiven wrote to all the Inveresk members in the area, suggesting to them that their loyalty was now to the new St Ninian's and inviting them to ask for their disjunction certificates, thereby giving away at a stroke several elders as well as the Guide Captain and Sunday School leaders, all of them first class people.

When my time at St Ninian's came to an end, I worked for a further year in another part of the old parish of Inveresk, at Whitecraig which was a mining village, and Smeaton, a tin hut of a church which served the folk who lived and worked on the estate of Carberry (still at that time the home of Lord and Lady Elphinstone). Again the limitations on my ministry became obvious: I could lead Sunday worship and look after the people through the week, but for the Sacraments and marriages I had to call in Dr Stiven.

It was during my time at Whitecraig and Smeaton that it was decided by the General Assembly that if deaconesses were to be conducting worship regularly they should be properly authorised to do so, and that meant being "licensed

37

to preach". The Deaconess Board approached me to ask that I apply for licence: I replied that I was not happy with the distinction being made between the ministry of the Word and that of the Sacraments, which have always been regarded as belonging together, but that if that was what the Assembly wanted me to do I would comply. I was accordingly taken on trials for licence by the then Presbytery of Dalkeith, duly licensed at a service in Inveresk Church and given a Certificate of Licence from which the usual words about being a probationer for the holy ministry had been deleted. (Twenty-one years later the Presbytery of Edinburgh made that good and gave me a certificate which declared me to be a probationer for the ministry, but deleted the phrases about being licensed to preach the gospel.) Preaching at my Service of Licensing in January 1957, Principal John Baillie said that this was perhaps to be seen as a step towards further opportunities that might later open up. I also was inclined to think that although this licensing of those who were not proceeding to the ordained ministry was anomalous, it was possibly to be welcomed as a step forward. It is often through anomaly that the Church moves, doing a new thing and tidying up the situation afterwards.

In 1958 I was asked to take up a post as tutor at St Colm's College where, at that time, the Church trained men and women for overseas service and women for deaconess service in Scotland. I really had to intention of being a teacher in a college setting; but rather to my surprise the Chairman of the College Board, Dr George Gunn, put it to me that I owed a debt to St Colm's and with my qualifications I had some sort of an obligation to join the staff. That was, I suppose, his way of getting me to think seriously about the offer, which I did, and finally accepted.

St Colm's was originally the Women's Missionary College of the United Free Church; there was added the training of Church Sisters from 1916 onwards, and it remained a women's training college until shortly after I had myself been a student there in 1951-52. Then the Overseas Council began to use the College for training men as well as women going abroad as missionaries. When I was appointed in 1958, the Principal was Miss Jean Fraser who had worked previously as Youth Secretary, first for the British Council of Churches and then for the World Council of Churches.

Jean Fraser was a great Principal: unassuming and entirely without pompousness, her worth was, in my opinion, never fully recognised by the Church of Scotland. This was probably because St Colm's, even though it was the Church's one and only college, was rather a backwater; it was after all a women's college in origin if not now in fact, and that inevitably (though no doubt unintentionally) put it on the sidelines. But Jean had a width of vision and a sense of purpose which ensured that St Colm's continued to be what it had always been, a place where all the barriers came down and where there was a true microcosm of the Church. Within the College there was a unity which transcended the segregations so common in the Church: ministry and laity, male and female, home and overseas mission. There were always residents from many other parts of the world as living reminders of the dimensions of the World Church. I think it would be true to say that, although in recent years St Colm's has expanded considerably into new fields of education, the Church at large is still scarcely aware of the great asset it possesses in this institution.

My appointment was to teach Christian Doctrine, some New Testament studies, and the practical training of deaconess students. In those days much of our teaching was still in the form of lectures and essays, although there was also a good deal of group work. One of the enduring traditions of St Colm's was that everyone — students and staff, ministers and lay people — took their share both in leading worship and in participating in group Bible Study. Being a residential college there was also stress on learning the art of living together.

I enjoyed my time on the staff of St Colm's. It was for me very much a time of learning as I tried to clarify my own thoughts on what I was supposed to be communicating to others, and as I (for a second time) lived and worked in this community which is such a powerful factor in creating the fellowship which deaconesses enjoy with each other.

When I had been three years in this post, the University of Edinburgh announced that it was intending to make an appointment to the new post of Assistant Chaplain to the University, and the then Chaplain, the Rev James Blackie, asked me to consider applying. The idea was that it would be good if he could have a woman colleague; I was interested to try this new venture and was in fact appointed for a three-year term. It was a very challenging experience. We worked from the old Chaplaincy Centre in Forrest Road (now the Bedlam Theatre, named after the old Bedlam or lunatic asylum which used to stand on that site); services and discussions of all sorts were held there, and we did our best to be available to students and staff throughout the whole University community — not easy with such a rapid turnover of students and such large numbers. The chaplains worked very much as a team: as well as Jim Blackie and myself, who held University appointments, there were full-time chaplains for Roman Catholic, Anglican and overseas students. I was the only woman and the only one not ordained, and it was in this context that I really began to think seriously that this was not an ideal situation, and that if I had been a man I would have been ordained long ago. The consequences of these thoughts we shall explore in the next chapter.

One incident may serve to highlight the problem. It was the custom to hold one University Service each term in St Giles' Cathedral, of which the minister was the Rev Harry Whitley. My role, along with the Anglican Chaplain, was usually to receive the offering and lay it on the table, and Dr Whitley had no problem with that. But on one occasion

Jim Blackie was suddenly struck down with lumbago on a Sunday afternoon at the close of a University Mission. The Missioner, Canon Max Warren of the Church Missionary Society, was due to preach in St Giles' that evening and Jim to conduct the service. When he heard that I was to lead the service, Dr Whitley absented himself and protested to the Chairman of the Chaplaincy Committee and the Principal of New College. We had a great service with a challenging sermon, but relations between the minister and the chaplaincy were very strained in the ensuing weeks. When I attempted to smooth things out by going to see Dr Whitley, he informed me that I had undone all that he had attempted to do in St Giles' in teaching the *men* of the congregation that they were priests in their own households; and that it was "not possible" for women to lead prayer in public. Why this was an impossibility was not very clear, but it was evident that this minister had very deep-seated problems with the whole concept of a woman leading worship. This attitude was by no means typical of the ministry, but to encounter it head-on like this was bound to be painful.

At the end of my three-year appointment the question was whether to accept the University's invitation to continue for another three years. I was finding it quite difficult, however, to work with Jim Blackie, the Chaplain. Much as I liked him as a person, our approaches to the task were rather different: it seemed to me that for him all questions were open questions and therefore up for discussion, whereas for me there were certain basic tenets of the faith on which the chaplaincy, representing the Christian presence in the University, should be expected to take a stand. Maybe I was not entirely fair to his position, but that is how I saw it. I decided not to continue, but to take a year off in order to travel. I had for many years wanted to go to India and this now seemed possible: to that was added an invitation to Ghana. The interest and significance of that trip I shall relate shortly.

* * * * *

During these first ten years as a deaconess (1954-64), I was actively involved in deaconess affairs. At this point we should look at some of the questions which were then at issue. We left the story at the point where in 1949 the General Assembly had agreed a new Scheme for the Order of Deaconesses, and the deaconesses themselves were already asking questions about office and function, about the meaning of 'Order' and about relation to the Courts and Committees of the Church. The Women's Home Mission Committee had been charged with a dual function — that of a 'Care Committee' and an employing committee — and they reported in 1954 that they found this unsatisfactory but were unable to decide who should look after those matters which related to the Order as a whole, and were therefore unable to present to the Assembly a scheme for the care of the Order. The outcome of this was that the Assembly appointed a Commission "to study the whole question of the Order of Deaconesses, to recommend a Scheme for the care of the Order and to report to the next General Assembly".

It seems amazing today that this Commission contained not one single deaconess in its membership: even in the 1950s it was evidently not envisaged that deaconesses could make an important contribution to the study, or not sufficiently important to warrant a departure from the usual Assembly committee structure of ministers, elders and 'women members', the latter meaning Committee ladies, not 'employees'. The Convener of the Commission was the Rev W Roy Sanderson of the Barony Church, Glasgow, and the members were influential and representative. They clearly worked hard and fulfilled their Assembly remit within the year, bringing a "Draft Scheme for the Order" to the 1955 Assembly.

But the Commission had not really addressed the fundamental questions which were in the minds of deaconesses, and it was only after work had been completed on the Draft Scheme that we were given an opportunity to make our comments on it. We took this invitation very seriously, discussing the Report in our local groups and at the Annual General Meeting in November to which Dr Sanderson was invited to hear our views. He was, I think, quite taken aback by the strength of feeling and opinion among the deaconesses that the Commission had failed to tackle the basic issues and that therefore we could not give unqualified approval to the Commission's finding. After a full discussion at the AGM we submitted a paper to the Commission setting out "a general consensus of opinion among the deaconesses of the Church".

This paper maintained that "the whole question of the Order of Deaconesses" could not be resolved until the following questions had been posed and answered: "(a) what is the 'office' of a deaconess in the Church?; (b) what is the 'diaconate', or particular ministry, to which deaconesses are called, and to which they are commissioned by the Church? and (c) what does the Church of Scotland mean when it speaks of an 'order' of deaconesses?" As a starting-point for the answering of these questions, we proposed the following thesis: "The word 'deaconess' both in the New Testament and in the history of the Church refers to an office in the Church. Hence, the 'order' of deaconesses must refer to an order of ministry in the Church, and not to any voluntary association, group or sisterhood of Christian women".

This proposition was one that I had worked on in collaboration with others and which I developed in a paper which we submitted to the Commission, and they in turn submitted it to the General Assembly as an Appendix to their 1956 Report. In this paper I sought to make the fundamental point that the Church should clarify its mind as to how it wanted to define or describe the office of deacon or deaconess, giving due regard to New Testament sources, the tradition of the Church and the intention of Dr Charteris and the Assembly of 1887. I then pointed out the ambivalence of the term 'order' in the usage of different branches of the Church. With reference to deaconesses it was used, for example, in the Church of England to denote an order of ministry to which women may be admitted by ordination which gives them a status in the Church. But it was also used on the continent of Europe, and especially in Germany, of the great Orders of Deaconesses which were conceived as religious orders or sisterhoods organised apart from the territorial Church and its parochial ministries. This second concept had been explicitly rejected by Dr Charteris on the ground that this did not represent the mainstream teaching of the Church on the diaconate. If we claim continuity with what the General Assembly established in 1887, then we should be clear that what is at stake is the office of deaconess as "an integral part of our Church system" (Charteris): they owe to it their standing and powers; and they have a right to ordination from it. The paper went on to conclude from this that the deaconess was the servant of the whole Church (not merely of the women's section or of any Committee of the Church), and that they should be given a place, as the third order of the Apostolic Ministry, with ministers of the Word and Sacrament and ruling elders, in the Courts of the church. The paper was remitted for consideration to the new Committee on the Order of Deaconesses (1956) and became part of the agenda of the Policy Sub-Committee which continued to keep policy issues before the main Committee over the next years.

This was possibly the best outcome we could expect. I had been in correspondence with Roy Sanderson throughout 1955, and I should want to make it clear that he was consistently courteous and helpful, and that his whole intention was to do what was best for deaconesses. But after meeting with us in November 1955 he was faced with a dilemma: whether to get the Assembly to adopt a revised Scheme for the Order which would provide for deaconess participation for the first time and for further policy discussions in the future, or to delay the whole process until the questions we were raising could be resolved. The former was no doubt the only practicable way forward. We had therefore to be content with what seemed to us to be yet another interim Scheme, recognising that it did make considerable advances: it set up the Deaconess Council as a forum in which deaconesses could discuss their own affairs and questions of wider import, and it set up the Committee on the Order of Deaconesses on which deaconesses were to be represented and which was to be directly responsible to the General Assembly.

Before leaving this 1955-56 debate, I append two footnotes. The first is that Presbyteries and Committees had also been asked to comment on the proposed scheme: of the former, several expressed dissatisfaction on the ground that the fundamental issues had not been addressed, and of the latter the comment of the Foreign Mission Committee (as it then was) was remarkable for its frankness: "The Commission's Report on the Order of Deaconesses is a painstaking, conscientious and brave attempt to deal with what is fundamentally an impossible task and a sub-Christian question remitted to it by the General Assembly, i.e. to make arrangements for whole-time, consecrated women servants of the Church, deaconesses, *outwith* the main official and constitutional life of the Church".

The second footnote concerns my first brush with authority. On 1 December the *British Weekly* published an article with the deplorable headline "What to do with women" by "Colin Craig", in which the author wrote that it appeared from newspaper reports of what I had said at the AGM of the deaconesses that I was "impatient — and discontented with the present state of affairs"; he went on to ask the curious question as to why, with my qualifications, I should be "satisfied with enrolment in the Order of Deaconesses of the Church of Scotland" and to suggest that

I was "after" the ordination of women to the eldership. The whole topic was further clouded in his article by being linked with the Overture proposing that certain deaconesses should be licensed to preach, which was at that time before Presbyteries and on which neither I nor any other deaconess therefore had made any public comment. I might have ignored this piece of rather irresponsible journalism had it not been for the fact that I knew 'Colin Craig' to be none other than the Rev William Smellie, minister of St John's Kirk, Perth, Convener of the Home Board and therefore my employer. I was, naturally I think, distressed that the Convener of the Home Board should write in these terms under a pseudonym and on the basis of press reports. On the advice of Dr Jack Stevenson of *Life and Work*, the official magazine of the Church of Scotland, I wrote to Mr Smellie and to the officers of the Women's Home Mission to put the record straight with regard to the attitude and opinions of the deaconesses' annual meeting. Mr Smellie replied that "I have made it my business to read the article in *British Weekly* to which you refer" (!), and that he had sent on to the Editor parts of my letter. My letter had been written to my employer and not to the press, and I was angry that it had been passed on in this way; I did not think further press coverage of the rather complex issues would be helpful. However, 'Colin Craig' in the December 15 issue of *British Weekly* offered "a sincere and unqualified apology" for misrepresenting my views and quoted extensively from my letter to Mr Smellie which may well have clarified things for readers. Apparently it did, for 'Colin Craig', admitted he was now "much more fully apprised of what Miss Lusk and her fellow deaconesses are 'after' ".

This whole episode did not exactly boost my confidence in the Home Board, whose convener should certainly have made it his business to be acquainted with the deaconesses' comments on the Report of the Commission rather than writing in the press under a pseudonym. Such misuse of power by influential men in the Church I was to encounter later, and it was always hurtful. This was in contrast to the helpfulness of Roy Sanderson who, as convener of the Commission, went to great lengths to enter into discussion with us once he realised that we had questions to ask and a point of view to express. The other encouraging factor was the common mind which we were discerning among ourselves. One of the most senior deaconesses, previously a Church Sister, writing to Dr Sanderson said "I would like to emphasise the fact that I have never known our combined group to be as unanimous as they were last Friday (i.e. at the AGM). You can take it that we are solidly behind Mary Lusk in all the points that she raised, and that we have not come to this viewpoint all in a day". In other words, I was not stirring up the deaconesses as some people maintained, but merely helping to articulate views already held. That was certainly how I saw it.

* * * * *

I have written in the previous chapter of my experience as a youth delegate to the World Council of Churches Assembly at Evanston, USA. This was the beginning of a whole series of marvellous opportunities to participate in the wider affairs of the Church while serving as a deaconess. These may not be strictly relevant to my main theme which is concerned with ministries in the Church of Scotland; and yet such experiences are certainly formative for anyone, and I should like to think that I have been enabled by them to bring a certain width of vision to the problems of our own Church.

After Evanston I was a member of the Inter-Church Relations Committee of the General Assembly, and then in the 1960s of a series of Anglican-Presbyterian Conversations, bringing together representatives of the Church of England, the Church of Scotland, the Presbyterian Church of England

and the Episcopal Church in Scotland. The Convener in both cases was the Very Rev Dr Archie Craig, who provided a memorable lesson in ecclesiastical statesmanship and in high principle when sadly he felt compelled to resign when the Assembly rejected the so-called "Bishops' Report". Another great ecumenical churchman of the time was Dr Robert Mackie, who had worked with the World Council of Churches in Geneva and was now back in Scotland. He invited me to be Secretary of the planning committee for the first Scottish Faith and Order Conference at St Andrews in 1963, of which he was Chairman, quite the best chairman I have ever known with great skills in holding diverse elements together and keeping everyone happy. The St Andrews Conference was in preparation for Nottingham 1964, the first Faith and Order Conference for all (non-Roman) churches in Britain, which I also attended.

Other memorable experiences were provided by my participation in the World Alliance of Reformed Churches as a member (the only woman) of the European Executive Committee which took me to Zürich, Warsaw, Budapest, Torre Pellice in the north Italian valleys, Frankfurt and other places. Perhaps the most exciting was when the Alliance appointed me as one of their representatives to the Laity Congress of the Roman Catholic Church in Rome in 1967. This was a follow-up to the Second Vatican Council and was an astonishing worldwide gathering of lay people, among whom I felt almost entirely at home, having been kindly absorbed into the Scottish delegation.

But perhaps the most significant of my international contacts were through the World Federation of Deaconess Associations (now the World Federation of Diaconal Associations and Sisterhoods). I attended international conferences at Uppsala, Berlin, Edinburgh (see chapter VII) and Helsinki; I served for eleven years on the Executive Committee, and for a number of years edited the English edition of the Newsletter. The value of the World

Federation, which originated in a Dutch initiative of reconciliation after the Second World War, lay in the fact that it brought into dialogue deaconesses of the continental motherhouse pattern with those of us who claimed to belong more closely in the official structures of the Church, as argued above; those whose task was in the main nursing and serving in large caring institutions with those of us who worked in parishes. This was undoubtedly mutually enlightening and beneficial.

Yet another opportunity of sharing in the World Church came my way in 1964-65. Hearing that I was intending to visit India after leaving the University Chaplaincy, the Rev Colin Forrester-Paton, one of our missionaries in Ghana, invited me to spend a month there on the way, to advise the Presbyterian Church about the training and deployment of deaconesses. After an intensely interesting month touring the country and visiting congregations and institutions, I reported to the Synod of the Presbyterian Church. My advice was to continue in the pragmatic approach which they had already adopted and train women (in a variety of marital status — there were very few single women) as parish workers, making use of the traditional women's skills of homecraft and child care, hygiene and cookery, as well as the churchly skills of Bible knowledge and teaching of the faith. Four such deaconesses had already been commissioned and I was able to bring this fledgling group into the fellowship of the World Federation.

In India I took part in a conference of the Order for Women of the Church of North India; taught for a month in Madras in the Church training college for women, Christa Seva Vidhyalaya; and met with Sisters of the Order for Women of the Church of South India, the aim of which was to bind together in fellowship educated women who were serving in a variety of ways in Church and community.

On the basis of this very limited foray into the life of what were then called the Younger Churches, I had the temerity to respond to an invitation from the World Council of Churches to contribute to a study booklet on *The Deaconess* (WCC Studies No 4, 1966). Having described what I had found in Ghana and India, I suggested that the development of women's ministry or deaconess service should be allowed to evolve in response to needs perceived; that such a pragmatic approach is possible for the diaconate in a way that it is not for the ordained ministry; and that Churches should be free to develop alternative ministries in forms suitable to their own situation. I think I should still stand by that today.

★   ★   ★   ★   ★

In 1960 my father died, a great release from a long and debilitating illness. We were able truly to give thanks for a life so well and fully lived. To the end he was reading his Greek New Testament every day, learning more and more of the mystery of God. In his retirement two subjects had continued to exercise his scholarly mind. One was the mystery of the Atonement, on which he read widely, pondered long and wrote wisely. The other was the Unity of the Church about which he cared passionately: his studies of Ignatius, the second century Father of the Church, and of the whole question of forms of ministry in relation to Church unity show an erudition not altogether common among parish ministers. Yet that was his calling. He was a much loved preacher and pastor, and fulfilled his calling happily and faithfully over many years.

For me he was a saintly example, a loving support in all I tried to do. Since his death I have always thought — I trust rightly — that he would have approved of the further steps I sought to take. He was not there when I petitioned the General Assembly, but I was pretty sure that he was with me in spirit.

V — Petition to the General Assembly

At 2.30pm on Saturday May 26 1963 I stood at the Bar of the General Assembly of the Church of Scotland to present my petition asking the Assembly to test what I believed to be my call to the ministry. When the Assembly met over a period of ten days, as it used to do, and Saturday was normally a half-day session, this was later said to be the longest Saturday session in living memory. Nobody went out for lunch, according to *The Scotsman*, and at 2.30pm the Hall and the public galleries were still well-filled. The Moderator himself, Professor J S Stewart, insisted on remaining in the Chair, determined to be in charge when my case came up. His presence, as a friend and as an eminently fair-minded chairman, helped somewhat to alleviate the extremely daunting situation in which I found myself.

That moment and the ensuing fifteen minutes of speaking to the Assembly were a watershed in my career. They labelled me for life as the woman who petitioned the General Assembly or, more usually, the woman who "led the fight" for women's ordination. The question might well then be asked as to how in the world I got myself into that frankly terrifying position. The answer is that I did not take on the role of petitioner at the Bar lightly, but rather as what seemed to be the inevitable and necessary outcome of a process of inner conviction and outward consultation.

A "deaconess licensed to preach" was the category of ministry in which I found myself. I had already expressed certain misgivings about this rather hybrid category. It was not of my choosing, but was the stage which the Church's thinking had reached. If it was anomalous, then perhaps it was also a pointer to growth and movement. So there was beginning to be borne in on me the realisation that this was perhaps not the last word of the Church on the matter and that it might be right to test out the Church's willingness to take a further step. The task of Assistant Chaplain in the University of Edinburgh seemed to provide the opportunity for that further step, since it required me to work within a team of chaplains all of whom had full scope to exercise their ministry, whereas mine was limited.

Over a number of months I consulted people whose experience and wisdom I valued — Dr Robert Mackie (whom I mentioned earlier), Dr Roy Sanderson (a former Moderator of the General Assembly) Dr Elizabeth Hewat (a distinguished professor) and others. Although we all knew that any member of the Church can bring a Petition to the General Assembly, the question was whether my facing the Church with my personal plea would help or hinder the process of theological decision-making which would be necessary to make possible the ordination of women. My advisers led me to believe that to personalise the issue by confronting the Church with a well-qualified candidate would be helpful. Minds would at least have to be concentrated.

Elizabeth Hewat (who held the degrees of MA, BD, PhD and DD) was Professor-Emeritus of History in Bombay, and one who might well have been ordained many years before had it been possible. She had in fact in 1926 persuaded four Presbyteries in the United Free Church to overture their Assembly to allow women to be licensed and ordained, but to no avail. She gave me her considered opinion in a letter in July 1962. "The more I think of it, the more I think you should go ahead and petition the General Assembly." She gave four reasons for this: "1. As long as we women don't do anything about ordination, people may conclude that we are satisfied with the present position. 2. If one woman petitions and says she has received a call from God — that is a fact that has to be taken seriously. 3. It is just nonsense to say it may be harmful ecumenically. The Church never moves all together on one issue. One Church leads, and then others take courage and follow. 4. Principles and spiritual convictions again and again have to be personalised and made manifest in one person before they seize the imagination and conscience of most people."

Thus encouraged, I consulted the then Principal Clerk of Assembly, the Rev James Longmuir, who was consistently courteous and helpful, explaining that I would have to pay for my own petition (in the event, a printer's bill for £6. 9s. 6d!) and guiding me through the correct form and wording for such a petition. Further, I informed the Convener of the Deaconess Board, the Rev Ian Dunlop, of my intention. His response was that he, too, thought it good that the Assembly should have a specific case before it to help it to face the situation.

★　★　★　★　★

The fact is that the issue of women's ordination had been before the Church previously, but over the years it had been somewhat concealed under the curious heading "The Place of Women in the Church", and the question of ordination to the ministry had taken second place in the Church's deliberations to the rather less thorny question of the eligibility of women in other spheres.

As long ago as 1916, in the United Free Church, a Report was submitted from the Committee on the Recognition of the Place of Women in the Church's Life and Work. This Committee made proposals for women in Assembly Committees and Deacons' Courts, women associated with Kirk Sessions and women as Church Sisters; but was of the opinion that it was "not the time to raise more fundamental proposals". The Assembly concurred with that opinion, but the debate must be remembered for contributions by those who thought all the barriers should come down, for example Professor H R Mackintosh, who said "People ask, 'Where are you going to draw the line?'. Why draw the line? God has not drawn the line for us."

Ten years later, also in the United Free Church, the overtures from four Presbyteries, already referred to, were received by their General Assembly. They asked that the Assembly should initiate legislation declaring women eligible for admission to Colleges as regular students (i.e. candidates for the ministry), who on completion of their course might be licensed to preach and ordained to the Ministry. And it was averred that there was "no adequate reason why any sex disqualification should be retained". An interesting debate ensued, most of it on a high level; but it also threw up such gems as "A woman's supreme heritage is motherhood", and the opinion that the admission of women to the ministry would increase the scarcity of men "for it would discourage a certain class of men of virile type from entering the profession (Hear, hear)." The proposal to appoint a Committee "to consider the whole matter in all its implications" was finally withdrawn in favour of the agreed motion that "the Assembly did not feel that the present time was opportune for taking any steps along the lines suggested by the Overtures".

1916 was "not the time"; in 1926 the time was not "opportune". The next attempt was made in the re-united Church of Scotland.

In 1931 the Marchioness of Aberdeen, Lady Balfour of Burleigh, Lady Frances Balfour and 335 other women brought a Petition to the General Assembly "on behalf of themselves and other women in full communion". This splendid petition went straight to the heart of the matter with no beating about the bush, and no suggestion that the Assembly might want to proceed step by step.

> "Your Petitioners desire that the barriers which prevent women from ordination to the ministry, the eldership and the diaconate [i.e. deacons' courts] be removed so that the principle of spiritual equality for which the Church stands be embodied in its constitution.

"Your Petitioners believe that the continued exclusion of women from these offices is contrary to the mind and teaching of Christ, and that it limits the operation of the Spirit of God.

"Your Petitioners are convinced that women no less than men are called to the ministry of the Church, and that the Church is the poorer by reason of women being debarred from the ministry as well as from the other offices."

Lady Aberdeen, who in the last quarter of the 19th century had displayed advanced views on the education and betterment of women, especially farm servants and domestic servants, was now a greatly respected figure in her seventies. She was clearly listened to with close attention by the Assembly as she pled that young women graduates should not be debarred from service in the Church, and that women should share in Church government and work on equal terms with men. She called in support St Paul who had said that in Christ there is neither male nor female and who, she suggested, might well have recommended Priscilla, Phoebe and other women for the eldership.

On the motion of Principal Alexander Martin, seconded by Dr John White, the Assembly agreed by an overwhelming majority to receive the petition, to recall with thankfulness "the devoted labour of women" in various spheres and to remit the petition to a Special Committee of thirty (one-third from women's committees and organisations) "to examine carefully the various questions raised by the petition and to report to next General Assembly".

Henceforth the petition came to be known as the "Petition Anent the Place of Women in the Church" (a phrase taken from the sixth and last paragraph of the petition) and the Special Committee was given the same title. Its remit was therefore a wide one and was not sharply focussed on the issue of ordination. Indeed the Convener, Professor Archibald Main of Glasgow, admitted to the Assembly in 1932 that the Committee had not had adequate discussion on the question of ordination, and said in 1933 that there was no agreement in the Committee and therefore they were not prepared to recommend that women become eligible for ordination. In 1934, after Presbyteries had disapproved (by a majority of 50 to 16) the proposal to admit women to the eldership, the Committee reported on the question of ordination to the ministry as follows: "In view of the votes of the Presbyteries upon the crave anent the Eldership, the Committee submits that no useful purpose would be served by further discussion of this subject at the present time".

There was in the event no deliverance of the Assembly on the question of the ordination of women, and in the course of the four Assemblies at which the matter was before them there had been remarkably little theological consideration given to the merits or otherwise of the case. The admirably sharp focus of the original petition and its spiritual and scriptural basis had scarcely been addressed and no adequate answer had been given to the petitioners.

However, all was not lost. In the course of the four years in which the subject had been before the Church, however obliquely, a number of hopeful signs emerged. In their 1933 Report, the Committee included, as appendices, papers which began to tackle the biblical and theological issues involved. The Rev J Cromarty Smith's paper against ordaining women does not question the spiritual equality of men and women, but asserts that spiritual equality does not imply equality of vocation or function. He finds in Scripture and in the whole tradition of the Church no evidence of women being admitted to the ministry and argues that departure from Catholic tradition and practice is not permitted. On the other hand, Dr James Weatherhead (grandfather of the present Principal Clerk) in his paper asserts "All the offices in the Christian Church should be open to women, because that is in accordance with the mind of Christ as that mind is revealed in the New Testament", and he cites Paul's dictum, already referred to, that "in Christ there is neither male nor female". The apostolic Church, he maintains, failed to grasp the mind of Christ, and women became subordinated in the Church. Dr Weatherhead concludes with the question: If a woman believes herself called and is trained and otherwise a satisfactory candidate, "why should the Church refuse her ordination?".

Another interesting line of thought, prompted by Dr John White's alternative proposals for giving women more scope without disturbing the peace of the Church by attempting to alter the law with regard to eldership or ministry, was that the scope of the Order of Deaconesses might be extended and developed. The Committee expressed this as reviving "the scriptural and primitive order of the ordained female diaconate", an *ordo clericalis* in the early Church. This would mean full theological training and "licence to exercise their gifts", in such fields as the preaching of the Word and the administration of Baptism.

Let the last word be with the Clerk, Dr James Harvey, who in seconding the Committee's deliverance in 1934 said, quoting his own words of eighteen years previously in the United Free Church, "There is no direct prohibition in our standards of the ordination of women, and there is a presumption that when the Church is ready freely and unreservedly to set women apart by ordination to any office to which they may be qualified, it may do so with the confident assurance of the blessing of the gospel of Christ in whom there is neither male nor female". That time he recognised, in view of the adverse vote of Presbyteries on the eldership, had not yet come. The Church had to wait a few years yet.

It was not until 1958, which brought the appointment of a new Committee on the Place of Women in the Church, that the issue emerged again into the cognizance of the General Assembly. This Committee was appointed as a result of Overtures anent Women in the Eldership presented by three Presbyteries in the Assembly of 1957, and sent down by that Assembly to all Presbyteries for their consideration. In 1958 the Committee on the Place of Women in the Church was instructed to examine the returns from Presbyteries, and to carry further the whole question of "the service of women in the Church". On the issue of ordination this Committee, like its predecessors, admitted that it was unable to come to a common mind and therefore said in 1960 that they would not consider it further. However this was not before Presbyteries had been instructed by the 1959 Assembly to give serious thought to "the theological and practical considerations underlying both the admission of women to the Ministry of Word and Sacraments and the existing tradition whereby this Ministry is confined to men". And the Committee themselves in 1959 had posed some sharp questions arising from the decision of the Church in 1956 to license duly qualified deaconesses as preachers of the Word. It is "difficult to say why certain Deaconesses, authorised to preach the Word and occupying comparable positions as assistants [i.e. comparable to that of male ordained assistants], should not similarly be ordained". Again, "If a woman maintains that she has received the call of God to the Ministry of Word and Sacraments, on what grounds does the Church admit her call to the Ministry of the Word and not of the Sacraments?". And, "the question is raised of what exactly is involved in the capacity of a woman to preach the Gospel and her incapacity to celebrate the Sacraments of the Gospel".

The issue now passed to the Panel on Doctrine. The Panel was set up by the General Assembly in 1960 and its first remit was to bring forward a Statement on Ordination. On the discharge of the Committee on the Place of Women in the Church the Panel was asked to consider the whole question of "Women in the Church". But in 1961 they reported having set up a Sub-committee on Ordination, and the question of women would have to wait. In 1962 the Panel "does not expect to take up the remit concerning women in the Ministry for some time".

In fact, they were better than their word, and the following year produced a Statement on Ordination to the Holy Ministry which was sent to Presbyteries for comment; and the Convener, Dr Roy Sanderson, expressed in the Assembly their readiness now to take up "the important matter of women in the Church". But that is to anticipate; for he said this in 1963 in the debate on my Petition.

The story thus far of the Assembly's attempts to bring to a conclusion the question of the admission of women to the ministry and the record of the handling of it by Committees of the Assembly did not inspire great confidence that this process would provide the way forward. It could be that what was indeed needed was that the Church be faced by a particular case of a woman candidate.

* * * * *

The Petition which I brought to the General Assembly of 1963, couched in the curiously archaic language of that august body, began with the words "Unto the Venerable the General Assembly of the Church of Scotland; Humbly showeth . . .". The Petition then rehearses the sequence of events which had brought me to this point — my Commissioning as a Deaconess, my fields of service over the past seven years, my licensing as a preacher of the Gospel, and then continues:

> That, being appointed a Chaplain in the University of Edinburgh, she submits that this represents a call to the ministry, and that her present appointment constitutes a sphere in which the full ministry should be exercised;

That, aware that in the tradition of the Church ordination to the ministry has been open only to men, your Petitioner submits that, in the light of modern biblical scholarship and interpretation, it can now be seen that the New Testament teaches an equality of men and women in Christ which makes untenable the continued exclusion of women from the ministry;

That she believes herself called of God to the Ministry of Word and Sacraments, and humbly begs that the Church will, in accordance with the practice of the Reformed Church, test her call, and if satisfied proceed to make possible her ordination to the ministry;

May it please your Venerable Court to take the necessary action to enable the appropriate Presbytery to proceed with the ordination of the Petitioner, or to do otherwise as your Venerable Court may think fit.

And your Petitioner will ever pray.

I was allowed fifteen minutes in which to present the Petition. I did this in a speech which was well received and which evoked so much interest both in the Assembly and afterwards that it should perhaps be recorded here in full:

Moderator, Fathers and Brethren, I present to you the Petition in my name, which you will find on page 103 of the Second Book of Cases.

This is a Petition for Ordination to the Ministry of Word and Sacraments. I am aware that in the normal course the Presbytery is the court to which a call to the ministry has to be submitted. But I have been advised that since I am a woman what I believe to be my call is thought to be of a special character, and that consequently I have to submit it in the form of a petition to the General Assembly. This I now do.

The fact that as a woman I should be required to show

special cause why I should be ordained appears to me a curious situation; for my plea is that as a person I may share in the whole ministry of the Church, and may therefore be eligible to be ordained to any particular ministry within the Church. This conviction I find shared by no less a body than the Special Commission on Ordination and the Ministry set up recently by the World Presbyterian Alliance. In a report issued a few years ago, they say, "The Commission wishes to say... that in principle it sees no reason why the ministry of women should be considered as a special category at all for, in the view of the majority of its members, it should go without saying that all that has been said of the Church's ministry herein applies equally to men and women".

This is my position. I do not regard the issue as a 'woman's question' nor as a fight for 'equal rights' nor even as a challenge to the Church. I am prompted simply by the awareness of a call to a service for which the authority of ordination is required.

I believe myself to be called of God to the Ministry of Word and Sacraments. It is difficult, I think, for anyone to say precisely how such a call comes. But this at least I can say: that it has come through an awareness of the work and mission of the Church and of the need, within the total ministry of the Church, for the ministry of full-time trained servants. When I first responded to this call, the Church said to me: "Be a Deaconess". This I did, with the fullest training I could get. I was duly commissioned as a deaconess and licensed as a Preacher of the Word; and I have found great scope and satisfaction in the service of the Church — as an assistant in a parish, as a lecturer in St Colm's College and now as Assistant Chaplain in the University of Edinburgh. I now find myself appointed to a task of a kind normally undertaken by an ordained minister, and this I ask the Church to recognise, and to give me for it the full authority of ordination.

Two points require to be amplified here before proceeding further:

The first is my licensing as a Preacher of the Word. And the second, my appointment as a Chaplain in a University.

1. In 1956 the General Assembly passed an Act which authorised the licensing of suitably qualified deaconesses as Preachers of the Word. Some of us at the time were not altogether happy about this; and when it was suggested to me by the Committee on the Order of Deaconesses that I should be licensed I agreed, but expressed to the Committee misgivings about the separation being made between Word and Sacraments. Further experience and thought have confirmed these misgivings: not only have I been aware personally of a certain tension and frustration inherent in a merely partial authorisation; but more important, I have become more convinced that theologically the two functions of ministry belong together and should not be permanently divorced the one from the other.

Last year the General Assembly recognised the office of deaconess as a distinctive office in the Church, complementary to, but in no sense to be equated with, the Ministry of Word and Sacraments. Does this not mean that the preaching of the Word, for which I have been licensed, has now to be seen as belonging properly within the total Ministry of Word and Sacraments?

2. My second point: In 1949 the General Assembly passed a Scheme for Deaconesses envisaging for deaconesses theologically qualified service in a wide variety of spheres, including service as Chaplains in Universities and Colleges. The vision of the 1949 Scheme brought me into the service of the Church. When in 1961 my term on the staff of St Colm's was

completed and I was intending to return to parish work, I was asked to take the appointment of Assistant Chaplain in the University of Edinburgh. This I did with the encouragement of the Committee on the Order of Deaconesses. However, in 1962 the General Assembly accepted the ruling of the Panel on Doctrine that a Chaplain was necessarily a Minister of Word and Sacraments, and that therefore a Deaconess could not serve as a chaplain but only as "an assistant in a chaplaincy". I submit that in fact my appointment as an Assistant Chaplain carries the functions for which in the case of a man ordination would be deemed necessary, and therefore I ask the Church to ordain me.

But it would be naive of me to suppose that the matter can be decided simply on the grounds that I believe myself to be called and that I am fully qualified and appointed to a ministry requiring ordination. It might be so in the case of a man, but in the case of a woman the whole weight of the tradition of the Church is against the ratifying of her call. It is not that the subordinate standards of the Church expressly prohibit the ordination of women; they do not. But by implication and by tradition women have been excluded, and therefore further argument is necessary.

This argument must clearly be theological. The question is all too often bedevilled by arguments sociological, psychological, biological, practical and the rest. No doubt some such arguments have their relevance, but it can only be a strictly limited relevance. The decisive argument for a Reformed Church can only be theological. We are concerned here with the New Testament doctrine of the Church and of ministry, and with the New Testament doctrine of the equality of the sexes in Christ.

I would submit that there is to be found in Scripture no theological ground for denying ordination to women.

If one takes the New Testament as a whole one sees that women played a full part in the service of the whole body, being accepted fully as persons by Christ Himself and then by His followers. Paul is often considered to be the stumbling-block here, with his injunctions to silence; but these should surely be taken against the background of far more general evidence of his acceptance of women in the Church — as his fellow workers and as leaders in prayer and prophecy in public worship — and all this based on the theological ground that in Christ there is no difference as to male and female.

Of course the Order of Redemption in Christ does not contradict the Order of Creation. Of course, men are still men, and women women, and we glory in it. There can be no question of women wanting to be like men and to take on anything that is shown to be a male function. But I have yet to be convinced that to preach the Word is to do something specifically masculine — if I were so convinced I should stop doing it; I fail to see how the ministry of the Sacraments belongs to men exclusively in virtue of their maleness; and if it be the exercise of discipline which is objected to in the case of a woman, then we have to remind ourselves that the only kind of government rightfully exercised within the Church is the authority of the Servant, and surely that kind of authority can never be held to be the prerogative of the male sex.

May I repeat — I am not concerned to usurp a male function. I submit rather that the function of ministry is a function which belongs to the whole body of Christ, to the whole Church in which men and women belong together. Within that body the particular ministry of Word and Sacraments is given to those who are called to it and equipped for it, and whose call the Church ratifies by ordination. I submit that there can be shown no adequate reason why this should not be true for women as for men. We, equally with you, fathers and brethren, are heirs of the promises, recipients of grace and of the Holy Spirit; and the onus of proof rests on those who would exclude us from the exercise of any form of the ministry of the Church.

More positively, it is not merely that there is no good reason against; there is surely very good reason for the Church welcoming the complementary service of men and women and their co-operation in all spheres of the ministry of the Church. We are concerned for the wholeness of the Church. Is not this wholeness maimed by the refusal to accept the gifts of mind, spirit and personality of men and women in all spheres including the ordained ministry? It would surely be for the good of the whole Church if there could be a complete and free acceptance of women as fully persons within the body of Christ and therefore an acceptance of their ministry as well as that of men in all realms of the life of the Church including the Ministry of Word and Sacraments.

We are concerned in another sense with the wholeness of the church, namely with the unity of Christ's church. It has been argued, and no doubt will be argued again, that although there may be no theological ground on which the Church of Scotland can refuse ordination to a woman, yet there are serious ecumenical grounds because such a step would impede our relations with other branches of the Church. Now this has certainly given me pause; for I am in a number of particular ways deeply committed to the search for the unity of the Church and to a vision of the Church Catholic in all places and all ages. But I believe it to be a specious argument. The Church can only grow into the unity which Christ wills for her as each separated branch of the Church is obedient to the truth as she sees it. And therefore it can only be right for any denomination representing, as it believes, the Church Catholic, to act in obedience to the guiding of the Holy Spirit, as He helps it to interpret Scripture.

Moderator, Fathers and Brethren, I finish where I began, by simply saying that I believe myself called of God to the Ministry of Word and Sacraments, and asking that this call be examined and dealt with in whatever way the Church may see fit.

According to *The Times* of Monday May 27, "It was obvious as soon as Miss Lusk had delivered the petition that she had gained the sympathy of most of the all-male assembly. On several occasions the Moderator, Professor J S Stewart, had to remind the fathers and brethren that the assembly was convened as a court and that applause was not permitted". Philip Stalker, Kirk elder and long-time reporter of the Assembly, wrote in *The Scotsman*: "None of us who were there will easily forget the occasion. There was nothing emotional about it, but her address — because of its unpassioned sincerity, its spirituality and the clear conviction of the speaker's call to a further service in the Church which only the Church could make possible — was very moving". And the Moderator, who with characteristic kindness took time to write to me on the Saturday evening, said: "I feel I want to tell you what a very deep impression you made as 'Petitioner' today ... You set the whole matter in its true perspective, and I for one found listening to you a deeply moving experience".

At the risk of appearing to have too great a conceit of myself, I record also comments on my speech made in the course of the debate by three very senior commissioners who might perhaps have been expected to have great difficulty with the request of the petitioner. The Rev F C Donald: "For the last fifty years I have been hearing petitions from the Bar ... and I can safely say, Sir, that I never heard a speech so clearly put, so logical all through and which ended when it came to the end". Sir James Simpson: "Just a few minutes ago we passed ten men into our Church [i.e. on petitions from ministers of other churches]. In my opinion in every way not one of them could hold a candle to the present Petitioner". Dr William Baxter of Dowanhill confessed that, after being for many years faced by this problem in the ministry "today I made up my mind that the barrier that prevents them from office should be uplifted ... I am utterly and enthusiastically in favour of this Petition".

Be all that as it may, it was not in fact at all clear what the Assembly should do with this petition. Those concerned with the legal niceties questioned the wording of what is called "the crave", i.e. the request for action in the last paragraph of the Petition; and questioned also whether a general principle could be decided on a particular case. Dr William McNicol (Convener of the Business Committee) even suggested that I was attempting to get the question "settled on a side wind", but was rebuked by the Moderator on the ground that such a tactic was certainly not in my mind. The Procurator (the Assembly's legal expert) advised: "It is perfectly competent for this crave to come before the Assembly and for the Assembly to treat it on its merits". He also made it clear that only the Assembly could take a decision. For although there was no Statute Law prohibiting the ordination of women, yet "there certainly is the practice of centuries. Of course, this has the force of Law".

The General Assembly then could address itself to the crave of the Petition; moreover, it had an obligation to do so because no one else could. But the question of the particular case and the general principle was not easily settled. The Rev W Paton Henderson submitted that "a general principle is always brought forward by a particular case". And in a powerful speech, the Rev Campbell Maclean said that in this matter "the Church has been all too clearly allowed the luxury of indecision and equivocation precisely because it was dealing with a general subject". The Church was now challenged by the particularity of the Petition: "How do we

67

deal with the claim of this particular woman's demands upon the Church?". Dr Roy Sanderson said that the Petitioner raised in an acute and responsible way the central issue, which was the possibility of a woman receiving a call and the testing of that call by the Church; that, rather than a theoretical discussion of women's place in the Church, was the question before them.

Nonetheless, Dr McNicol and the Rev Andrew Herron, Clerk to the Presbytery of Glasgow, insisted that the practice of centuries should not be set aside on a particular Petition, and moved that "the crave of the Petition be refused". On a vote this was overwhelmingly defeated. (It was not altogether clear that it was the legal point which really troubled Dr McNicol, since he also said he was sure he was "speaking for the great majority of the members of the Church of Scotland throughout the land when I say that they have no desire, now or at any other time, for women in the ministry".)

The Assembly was now faced with a choice of motions. Bill Paton Henderson moved in the following terms: "The General Assembly grant the crave of the Petition and instruct the Principal Clerk and the Procurator to draft an Overture to be sent down under the Barrier Act giving effect to the crave of the Petition". This would have been the bold response to "a significant and historical situation" called for by a number of speakers, among them Campbell Maclean, T M Donn, Murdo Ewen Macdonald and Sir James Simpson. According to Philip Stalker of *The Scotsman* "the dramatic texture of the occasion, the feeling that the Church was on the point of making a new decision in her history, began to build up".

Many of those who wanted to see the Petition granted in the end of the day nevertheless urged caution and proposed that the Church should give careful consideration to the matter before coming to a decision. Dr Baxter, declaring himself wholeheartedly in favour, urged that for the sake of the peace of the Church the Petition should be referred to the Panel on Doctrine. This was in accordance with the motion already proposed by Dr Roy Sanderson which was, "The General Assembly note with interest the crave of the Petition and are anxious that it, along with all its implications, should be carefully considered before a reply is given. They therefore instruct the Panel on Doctrine to give consideration to the Petition and its crave when it is dealing with the Place of Women in the Church and to report to next General Assembly".

On a vote being taken this was the motion that was carried. After the vote a Commissioner asked whether the Convener of the Panel on Doctrine would consider consulting with the Petitioner, to which the Convener, Roy Sanderson, replied, "The Panel on Doctrine will certainly be in touch with Miss Lusk".

*   *   *   *   *

I have no doubt that the Assembly took the right decision: it was right that the question which I had raised should be given serious theological consideration, and the expectation was that this would best be done by the Panel on Doctrine. The fact that the Panel on Doctrine led the Assembly into some rather strange territory is a matter for the next chapter.

But before leaving the General Assembly of 1963 I should want to look back from the perspective of nearly thirty years later and ask whether my arguments still hold. So far as I am able to judge, they do. I find, in fact, that I should want to stand by all of them, and I do not think that subsequent argument or events have led me to depart from any aspect of the case which I then put to the Assembly.

With regard to the question of whether it was right to put a particular case before the Assembly for its judgement, I believe firmly that it was. The issue was really not the legal one of whether a general question can be decided on a particular case. The issue was a theological one, viz. the priority of person over principle. The whole biblical revelation is of a personal God working through persons: the God of the Old Testament is the great I AM; Jesus said the truth is personal — "I am the Truth"; the Holy Spirit informs and indwells persons. Therefore the existential question is, has God called this person? Does He want him or her in the service of His Church? If so, then women can be called by God and the general principle is established.

"I believe I am called to the ministry." Such a statement rests on the knowledge of my baptism and of my salvation, as I tried to say to the Assembly. In the church where I was baptised, St Columba's Oxford, the font stood in the traditional position at the door, so there was no doubt that baptism was the rite of entry into the Church; and on the font my father had placed a card with the words of the Larger Catechism on 'the improving of our baptism', i.e. the lifelong duty of recalling, considering and drawing strength from our baptism. That has always meant much to me: the recollection that in infancy God put His Name upon me, made me incorporate in the body of Christ, called me to be His witness and servant. In Luther's words, *"Baptizatus sum"*. So far as I am aware, He made no distinction in this between me and my brothers. Nor can any distinction be made between men and women with regard to salvation. He came and He took upon Him human flesh: my flesh as well as that of any man. Therefore what right had men to exclude me from the privileges and duties of those who are being saved?

This is central to the New Testament, this common humanity in Christ, before God. Jesus spoke to and treated women directly and personally and with a freedom from the conventions of His time: He even called a woman to be the first witness to His resurrection. Arguments from omission — no women among the apostles, no women among the Seven of Acts 6, no sign of women among bishops and

70

elders — are bound to be inconclusive, because any attempt to assess the reasons for these omissions has to be speculative.

I have never actually pleaded 'equality' in the sense of sameness, though it is frequently assumed that this is what I am talking about. I do not think equality in that sense between men and women is a biblical concept: in fact, I do not know what it means. Rather I have pleaded what may be called 'spiritual equality', i.e. the notion of grace freely given to all, women and men alike. And therefore I have maintained that the onus of proof is on those who would *exclude* any from God's call, whether on grounds of sex or colour or race or whatever.

I personally have not wanted to be equal to men, which I find to be a meaningless idea. By the same token, in "wanting to be a minister" as some would put it, I am very clear that I am not wanting to be male or to perform a male function. That is one reason why I do not wear a clerical collar, which is a male form of dress. My position then, as now, was: I believe God wants me as a woman: prove to me that He cannot have me. I am not a man: I am different: I do not aspire to be a man: I want only to be given the chance to minister as a woman.

I have always thought it very strange that the Church should think it appropriate or even possible to sit round a table and discuss the subject quaintly called "The Place of Women in the Church". It is not dead yet, and it seems difficult for men to appreciate why I find it so strange. But the truth is that we — women — *are* the Church together with men; and therefore cannot have a place prescribed for us by the men of the Church. The wholeness or health of the Church demands that people see this: it demands a fuller and freer community of women and men in service at all levels. The fact that I had to lay my plea before an exclusively male Assembly meant that any consideration given to it was bound to be distorted and incomplete.

Finally, is there more to be said on the ecumenical question after all these years? In 1963, in response to Dr MacNicol's assertion that the Church of Scotland could not move on its own, Campbell Maclean asked "whether the Church's assets were to be frozen, her imagination smothered and no doctrinal issue discussed because they were always looking over their shoulder to see what other denominations were thinking about?". I have always thought it strange that certain speakers, then and since, have suddenly become filled with ecumenical enthusiasm when this, alone among issues, has been raised. I should stand by what I said in 1963, that "the Church can only grow into the unity which Christ wills for her, as each separated branch of the Church is obedient to the truth as she sees it". This means not only that the Church of Scotland was right to pursue the question according to her own lights, but also that in the intervening years we have had to look on powerless as other branches of the Church continue to agonise and struggle.

VI — Debate and Decision

From the perspective of the 1990's, it seems remarkable how much space the daily press gave to Church affairs in the '60s. The General Assembly's debate on my petition received front page coverage in *The Scotsman*, as well as lengthy reports inside that paper. *The Glasgow Herald* also dealt with it fully. *The Times* gave a fair account of it too, followed by a "Woman in the News" feature. England, apart from this, was not greatly interested in the situation, but the Australian *Melbourne Herald* carried an article. The source of this report was probably the *Ecumenical Press Service* or the *Reformed and Presbyterian Press Service*, both published in Geneva and both of which took note of the petition and debate. It was no wonder then that the petitioner found herself somewhat over-exposed.

Most of the press comment was sympathetic, though a columnist in *The Sunday Post* (the widely read Scottish family paper) headed his column "No, no, lassie, it'll nae dae" and went on to say that, speaking as a man, he did not think he could thole a woman preaching Sunday after Sunday; when she raises her voice she loses her dignity: how would she cope with standing at an open grave on a cold, wet day? Marrying people is a man's job, and he could not possibly unburden his soul to a woman. There was more, but this is enough to indicate how quaint some of the defence of the *status quo* sounds today.

A letter to *The Scotsman* from a minister's wife (one of a number of women who obviously found the whole idea difficult, and perhaps threatening to their husbands), started a correspondence which ran through most of July. She wrote that "Miss Lusk's petition filled me and, I believe, the majority of women in the Church with grave disquiet". She argued that "there are few sane people who will dispute that the man is the head of the house; then let the family of God have men at the top to minister to Christ's flock". Then came a curious variant on the usual plea that a woman finds her fulfilment in motherhood — this time in grannyhood: "Most of the women who seek this new status in the Church would in all probability, but for the terrible loss of life in the First World War, be grannies now, with all the absorbing interests this brings with it. This generation will pass ..." Actually I and my generation were not yet born in the First World War: that apart, it is interesting that such a view of 'women's place' was still being voiced at that time. The further letters were fairly evenly balanced for and against, with fairly predictable points being made.

Meantime, my own mailbag was mostly from friends and acquaintances. Some were not known to me — a young lawyer in Ceylon and a lady in Australia, for example. I also received letters of support from such bodies as the Anglican Group for the Ordination of Women and the (Anglican and Free Church) Society for the Ministry of Women in the Church. Of all the letters that I received, I was perhaps most moved by one from my father's oldest friend, Lord Elgin, who wrote, "I have always felt that the greeting contained in your name 'Mary' as recorded in St John 20:16 is one of the most precious words in the Bible and by the action you have taken in presenting this case, you have most closely fulfilled the instructions contained in the next verse of St John's Gospel". ("Go to my brethren and say to them, I am ascending to my Father and to your Father, to my God and your God", John 20:17.)

One of the people who had asked for a copy of my speech was Jim Michael, a Highland elder and a well-known, kenspeckle, kilted figure in the Assembly and in many ecumenical gatherings. A month later he wrote, "Having read your speech quietly more than once in the peace of the hills, I think this is one of the great historic documents of our Church and I am deeply grateful to God for allowing me to be in the Assembly that afternoon. There is something

74

incredibly uplifting in it — the marks of the Spirit".

These and like responses from senior churchmen were a great support when faced with adverse reaction, which was seldom of the same spiritual depth.

1963 closed with an ecumenical consultation in November on the ordination of women at Scottish Churches' House, Dunblane. This was called in response to a request from the World Council of Churches that papers on the subject, placed before the Faith and Order Conference at Montreal that year, should be discussed by churches all over the world. (These papers were later published by the WCC under the title *Concerning the Ordination of Women*, 1964.) I was abroad and not able to be at Dunblane, but they played a tape-recording of my speech, and listened to the experience of a woman who had served for 35 years as an ordained minister in the Congregational Union. The consultation agreed with the Faith and Order view that there was a need for fresh thinking on the theological, biblical and ecclesiological issues involved in the ordination of women; and that all churches, whether in favour of change or not, should engage in such study.

* * * * *

An impetus to the next stage of study within the Church of Scotland was given by Professor Tom Torrance who wrote an article in the February 1964 issue of *Manse Mail*, a publication sent out to all ministers of the Church of Scotland. The article, entitled "The Ministry of Men and Women in the Kirk", was in the form of seven theses designed to explicate the complementary nature of different ministries appropriate to men and to women, men being given a presbyteral function and women a diaconal one in the ministry of the whole Body. This 'economic ordering' of Christian service is founded on the same Scriptural basis as is Christian marriage: "In the family of creation there is a husbandly and a wifely ministry, which are mutually dependent and complementary. In the Church the presbyteral and diaconal ministries are similarly related". The whole argument stems from thesis number 2 which reads: "The basic unit of creation is not the individual human being, male or female, but Man and Woman as one Man, conjoined by God to be one flesh". Professor Torrance goes on, "This affects equally the doctrine of marriage and the doctrine of the ministry of men and women in the Church". So far as the ministry is concerned, it transpires from a reply which Torrance gave to a response from Dr William Lillie in a later issue of *Manse Mail* that women are to serve in "unassuming, unpretentious and unofficial ministry, yet real and proper ministry", while men are appointed to bear official responsibility in the public ministry".

It would be fair to note that Professor Torrance has changed his position very considerably since 1964 and that he is now an enthusiastic advocate of the admission of women to the 'official' ministry of the Church. But the *Manse Mail* theses are important if we are to begin to understand what happened within the Panel on Doctrine in 1964; for thesis 2 is quoted almost word for word in the Panel's Report and the whole stance of the Panel appears to be very similar to that of Professor Torrance, as will be apparent when we reach that point.

In the meantime, I was awaiting the fulfilment of the Panel's undertaking that they would consult with me on what I believed to be my call. The Convener, Dr Sanderson, had circulated my speech to the Panel and had been good enough to inform me that a sub-committee, under the chairmanship of Professor J K S Reid, had been appointed to take up the matter of my petition and the wider issues involved. "Professor Reid will no doubt be getting in to touch with you, within the next two or three months, but the Panel certainly agreed to call you in at an early stage".

76

That was in a letter of July 1963. By the following February there had been no word, so I wrote to Dr Sanderson expressing concern that the Panel's Report to the Assembly must by then be at an advanced stage without any consultation with me having taken place. The result was an almost immediate summons to attend a meeting of the Panel, at which I was asked what I had to say. It was not a happy occasion. I thought that I had already spelled out my case fairly fully, and I was expecting the Panel's response to the case I had laid before them. This was not forthcoming, and the interview was over in ten minutes.

The Panel's Supplementary Report on "The Place of Women in the Church" was released to the press on May 18 and *The Glasgow Herald* devoted its first leader to the subject. "The Panel has submitted a report which no one in the Church, including the Panel, can find entirely satisfactory". This was partly because the report offered "two irreconcilable conclusions on the crucial question raised by the petition"; and partly because "the argument against the full ordination of women is put in terms which the ordinary Church member will find it hard to follow, if not incomprehensible". The writer goes on to suggest that the Church cannot avoid the possibility that God may be calling her to new things.

The Scotsman foresaw a lively debate in the Assembly, and published a letter from Dr Elizabeth Hewat, written "to prepare the minds of members of the Assembly" by reminding them of the important issues involved. On the morning on which the Report was to be submitted to the Assembly, namely May 27, *The Glasgow Herald* again carried a first leader from which it is quite evident that that paper's view was wholeheartedly in support of the petition which it felt should be accepted without further delay. These two leading articles in *The Glasgow Herald*, written obviously by a committed churchman, gave what many would have regarded as the intelligent layman's view of the matter, advocating that the Church must not let herself be paralysed by tradition.

But what did this Report of the Panel on Doctrine actually say? Why was it so "hard to follow, if not incomprehensible"? And why did the Panel offer two irreconcilable conclusions?

We are told that Professor Reid's working party having brought their report to the Panel, the Panel made it the basis for its own Report to the Assembly. So the full Panel evidently takes responsibility for what follows.

The Report sets out five Agreed Theological Considerations, of which the first four would seem to be unexceptional basic propositions, viz: 1. The Church is Apostolic; 2. All members of the Church have a ministry to discharge; 3. Within the general *diakonia* of the Church, a special ministry was instituted by the Apostles; 4. In creation, God's eternal purpose for man is revealed, and in redemption it is brought to fulfilment.

After these four propositions have been briefly expounded, there follows this paragraph:

> 5. *The basic unit of humanity is not the individual human being, male or female, but man-and-woman as one.* At creation "God created man in His own image; in the image of God created He him; male and female created He them" (Gen 1:27). In redemption "they twain shall be one flesh" (Matthew 19:5). Of course an individual is either a man or a woman. But the image of God is not reflected by the individual man or woman; it is not man without woman, nor is it woman without man that is made in the image of God, but man-and-woman. This relationship, as established at the creation and endorsed by dominical words as valid also in redemption, is the basis of the doctrine of Christian marriage *and also of the doctrine of the ministry of men and women in the Church.*

I quote these words in full (the italics are mine) because it seems to me that this highly eccentric piece of theology led the Panel seriously astray. It was apparently agreed by the whole Panel, including those who went on to draw conclusions which pointed towards the admission of women by ordination to 'the official ministry'. But Consideration No. 5 is taken up also by those of a contrary view and developed in what seemed to me and to many others a quite extraordinary argument. "In the order of creation, as already seen, neither man alone nor woman alone reflects the image of God. The image of God is, however, reflected when man while remaining a man is complemented by woman while remaining a woman. ... In the order of redemption, this difference is not superseded but reduplicated; the family or household of God, which is the Church, is constituted by man and woman, each complementing the other but each remaining what each is. Both therefore have their appropriate *diakonia* with the Church . . . In biblical teaching, the man bears the outer responsibility in official duty, and the woman provides the inner determination which shapes and governs the Christian economy". This view goes on: "This differentiation of complementary functions is the key to what otherwise is without discernible explanation ... The ministry of women (according to the New Testament) is complementary to the official ministry. If this pattern were devoid of assignable reason, it might be deemed to be variable. Based as it is on the whole pattern of the Scriptural understanding of the place of man and woman in the purpose of God in creation and redemption, it supplies the norm for all ages". The conclusion is that "To admit women by ordination to the official ministry is not only a contradiction of biblical and traditional practice, but a denial of the biblical man-woman relationship in favour of a relationship of identity which has no biblical foundation".

This, one of the two Alternative Views set forth in the Report, has the feel of desperation about it. Most people

79

reading it — and I should guess all women reading it — if they could understand what it was driving at, would dismiss it as bunkum. I should moreover hazard a guess that very few, if any, of those who put their names to it in 1964 would stand by it today. But I have quoted it because it contributed both to the confusion of the Assembly and to the frustration of those of us who were awaiting a decision. The Panel believed that the division of opinion in their own membership "would be reflected throughout the Church, and that it would be inexpedient to ask for a decisive vote on this matter at this juncture. Presbyteries should first of all be allowed to study the Report". But my problem was "What would the Presbyteries make of it?". And because the Panel on Doctrine wanted Presbyteries to discuss the Report, it proposed to the Assembly "that the Petition of Miss Lusk should be dismissed at this juncture".

My Petition was still 'on the table' in the sense that the 1963 Assembly had neither accepted nor rejected the Crave, but referred it for consideration to the Panel on Doctrine. This meant that I was invited to speak again to the 1964 Assembly and given five minutes to do so. I was joined on this occasion by a second Petitioner, Miss Margaret Allan, a deaconess licensed to preach, who also believed herself called by God to the Ministry of Word and Sacraments. Her Petition was down on the Order of Proceedings to be taken immediately after mine, both following on the Report of the Panel on Doctrine, on the last day of the Assembly, Wednesday 27 May.

Once again I stood at the Bar of the Assembly in the role of Petitioner, while the Assembly sat as a Court to determine the merits of my case. Because on this occasion the Assembly also had before it the Supplementary Report of the Panel on Doctrine on "the Place of Women in the Church", I took it that I was at liberty to comment on that report as well as to put my own point of view. Again, it is perhaps best to reproduce my speech in full as it expresses both these

80

aspects of what I had to say, and tries also to explain how uncomfortable any woman would have felt with the whole proceedings.

Moderator, Fathers and Brethren,

I am grateful for this opportunity to reiterate the plea which I made to last year's General Assembly, and to comment on the Report which the Panel on Doctrine has now submitted and which seems to me to be fundamentally mistaken and misleading.

I am not sure that I can convey to an all-male Assembly the pain which the whole attitude and the very title of the Report give to me as a woman, for it assumes that there is a certain definite and limited 'place' which is to be given to women in the Church. The truth is that we, together with you Fathers and Brethren, *are* the Church and there can be no question of *your* prescribing for *us* an 'appropriate' sphere. Perhaps the point can best be brought home by suggesting that you substitute the word 'men' for the word 'women' in the title of the Report and ask Presbyteries to consider the spheres of ministry appropriate to men in the Church. Ludicrous? Of course — but not more so than the proposal before you.

Last year I said that I believed myself called of God to the Ministry of Word and Sacraments and asked that the Church would test my call. This I would submit has not been taken into account adequately by the Panel on Doctrine. Instead they have given us a theoretical discussion with two incompatible conclusions about the relationship between male and female.

I have said that I believe myself called by God to the Ministry. The fact that my appointment as Assistant Chaplain in the University of Edinburgh comes to an end shortly does not invalidate my petition for I seek admission to a ministry which I should exercise wherever God may call me. On grounds which I gave to the Assembly last year, I am certain of an inner call but there must also be a human agent and this there cannot be within the Church of Scotland till the barrier be removed.

The issue must then be decided on the matter of principle and the principle here involved is that God can call a woman to the Ministry of Word and Sacraments, but I find that this is not adequately dealt with in the Report.

Is it or is it not, Fathers and Brethren, conceivable that by the promptings and circumstances which I indicated last year, God is telling me, a woman, that He requires my service in the Ministry of the Church? If not, then cause has to be shown where I am in error. When I was called before the Panel on Doctrine no cause was shown. In fact, no significant matter was raised in the ten-minute interview which the Panel granted me. Is good cause now shown in the Report why it must be thought impossible that God should so call a woman?

I think not — whether we examine the logic of the argument or the theology of the position taken (and here I confine myself to those parts of the Report which are agreed by the whole Panel).

There is no mention of the indivisibility of Word and Sacrament. Surely this is of crucial importance. If a woman is called, as has been admitted, to the Ministry of the Word, on what grounds is she denied the Ministry of the Sacraments? Twice over by a rather odd logical procedure, the Report (on page 2 and page 6) speaks of two functions of the Church and says that it is the second which is appropriate to women — and this evidently in virtue of their baptism. Why this peculiar logic which twice over relegates women to the second place, the second part of the Church's ministry as here described?

(The two functions of the Church given in the Report were 'worship' and 'taking counsel'. No 2 of the Agreed Theological Considerations contained these words: "Acts of worship culminate in the Holy Communion; acts of taking counsel are undertaken in collegiate courts of the Church, in the case of the Church of Scotland, Kirk Session, Presbytery, Synod and General Assembly. All baptised persons are members of the Church which corporately exercises a Royal Priesthood as it worships or takes counsel. It follows that all who are of age have a place proper to them, either directly or through representation, in the courts of the Church". It is not explained why it should not equally follow that "all who are of age have a place proper to them" in acts of worship which culminate in the Holy Communion.)

The reason evidently is theological, or perhaps anthropological. It seems to be based on a quite special doctrine of man, which quotes a word of Jesus relating to marriage and makes it normative for the whole order of redemption; a special doctrine of man which speaks of a mythical animal, a non-existent entity called 'man-and-woman as one' and maintains (so far as I can understand it) that while the first limb of this being, viz. man, can exercise the ministry on his own, the second, viz. woman, cannot.

This bears no relation whatsoever to what I find in the New Testament. There I find that we are all being conformed to the image of God in Christ in so far as we die and rise again in Him. I find no reference to the marriage relationship (which may or may not imply a priority of one partner to the other) as normative for the relationships of men and women to one another and to Christ. I find women being accepted fully as individuals whom Christ has redeemed and who may therefore conform to His image.

True, there is no explicit reference in the New Testament to a woman being ordained to what may be called the 'official' ministry. But nor is there any explicit reference to the baptism of infants. Yet we baptise infants, because there is no New Testament reference to their exclusion, and more important, because infant baptism is a necessary implication of the gospel of the divine initiative and grace. So also, I would plead with you to see that the removal of the barrier to the ordination of women is demanded by the gospel itself, because the call of God can no longer be thought to be restricted to the male sex; and you must, so far as it is in your power, give effect to the freedom with which Christ Himself has set us free.

So once again, Fathers and Brethren, I say that I believe myself called by God to the Ministry of Word and Sacraments, and I ask you to make it possible for that call to be ratified.

The debate which followed was by any standard tangled and unsatisfactory. What the Panel on Doctrine was proposing to the Assembly was (1) that their Report should be sent to Presbyteries for consideration and comment, replies to be sent in by 31 December; and in the light of those replies, a further Report would be submitted to the next General Assembly. (2) "In view of the fact that the principles involved in the Petition of Miss Mary Lusk for Ordination to the Ministry of Word and Sacraments are included in the Report for consideration by Presbyteries and for further Report by the Panel to next General Assembly, the General Assembly agree to dismiss Miss Lusk's Petition at this juncture." There were also two Notices of Motion on the Order Paper. The Rev W Grahame Bailey wanted to move that "The General Assembly thank the Committee for its report and declare its support for the view expressed in it in

84

Sections 12 to 15 (i.e. the second of the Alternative views) that there is no bar to the admission of women to the Holy Ministry. The General Assembly instruct the Principal Clerk and the Procurator to draft an overture to be sent down under the Barrier Act giving effect to this decision". On the other hand, the Rev Tom Balfour's motion would have put a stop to the whole process by simply asking the Assembly to agree to dismiss the Petition.

The Convener of the Panel, Dr Roy Sanderson, speaking on the five Agreed Theological Considerations, conceded that with regard to No 5 ("The basic unit of humanity is not the individual human being, male or female, but man-and-woman as one") "it is possible that the agreement was more formal than real, for in the end different conclusions were to be drawn". The Panel had attempted to set down how far they could travel together, but because they were divided in their conclusions and thought that this division of opinion reflected the situation in the Church at large, they considered that a decision on such an important matter "should not be rushed"; hence the proposal to consult Presbyteries, asking for comments by the end of the year "because of the urgency of this matter". With regard to my petition, "the Panel feels that the Petition has fulfilled its purpose and yet it does not want to dismiss it out of hand ... We suggest the Assembly should dismiss the Petition in a technical sense". (Dr Sanderson reckoned that my purpose had been to bring the matter before the Assembly, and that it was now firmly before the Church through the Panel on Doctrine Reports. But whether these Reports would face the Church with the question of my call was questionable.)

In any case, the merits of the case were soon lost sight of in a procedural tangle. Even before the Convener's speech, Dr Harry Whitley, the minister of the High Kirk (St Giles' Cathedral) in Edinburgh, protested that Grahame Bailey's motion was "out of order" on the ground that they had not had sufficient notice of this doctrinal matter. The Principal

Clerk replied that it was not out of order but would require a "suspension of Standing Orders". The point was that this being the last day of the Assembly there was, in fact, no time for the preparation of an Overture and its presentation to a later session of the Assembly. This was the position in spite of the fact that Mr Bailey had given notice of his Motion five days previously, and the Depute-Clerk had given a verbal assurance that the Motion was accepted. A move to suspend Standing Orders requires a two-thirds majority in the Assembly. When an attempt was made so to move in order that an Overture could still be prepared and introduced (even on the last day of the Assembly), there voted for 262 and against 231, not the required two-thirds majority.

This meant considerable frustration not only for Grahame Bailey who could not now put his motion to the House and his seconder, Dr Alan McArthur, (who was prepared to demolish the Panel's report as "coming before us with a mystifying farrago of pseudo-theological nonsense which absurdly misrepresents the biblical doctrine of creation"), but also the large number of members who evidently wanted to discuss the issue theologically and on its merits. There were several attempts to get the Assembly's agreement with Sections 12 to 15 of the Report, stating that there is no bar in principle to the admission of women to the ministry. "Out of order," Dr Whitley cries again, on the ground that this is a matter of doctrine. "How is it," asks Alan McArthur, "that we cannot talk about doctrine?" Again the Principal Clerk, when appealed to, advised that for the Assembly to express an opinion on this matter would not be out of order but would be inadvisable: "I do not think the Assembly should declare on one side or the other".

The Rev Tom Balfour thought the Assembly should. On the grounds that Presbyteries had had ample opportunity to discuss the matter and that the Assembly was the Supreme Court, a decision should be taken now. Because there was division in the Church, Mr Balfour argued "we have a remit from the Church to do nothing at this stage". (A curious argument indeed! Why should the Supreme Court accept such a remit from the Church?) His motion simply to dismiss the Petition and take no further action was, however, defeated.

Grahame Bailey and others who wanted the consideration of the petition to be taken further saw that the only thing for them to do was to support the Panel's Deliverance as being "the only way of keeping the matter open now". Mr Bailey assured the Assembly he would not 'cheat' by making the speech which he would have made in support of his motion, but pleaded vehemently with the Assembly to remember that the more they delayed in this matter, the more would other churches continue to ordain *our* women.

Alan McArthur made a final attempt not to have the Petition 'dismissed' by suggesting rather that the Assembly should 'continue' it. But the Clerk advised against this on the ground that the Assembly could not be expected to hear the Petitioner again and again. On a question from Dr Archie Craig whether I could renew my Petition at a future Assembly, the Moderator replied in the affirmative. And so, finally, the Deliverances proposed by the Panel were agreed, which meant that my Petition was 'dismissed at this juncture', and the Report was sent down to Presbyteries for comment.

The Assembly moved on to the second Petition, viz that of Margaret Allan, who was then put in an extremely awkward and daunting position. It was moved that, in view of decisions just taken, the Petition should not be received at all; but Margaret Allan was entitled to speak not on the merits of the case but only to give reasons why it should be received, i.e. in what way her case was different from mine. How she was expected to do this on the spur of the moment and in face of Points of Order (as before) from Harry Whitley and Tom Balfour was not very clear; but the Convener of the Business Committee ensured that she should at least be given a hearing. So she proceeded to try to convey to this all-male gathering the struggle and pain involved in obedience to a Church which denied her call. When asked by Dr James Stewart from the Chair whether she wished to continue, Margaret wisely replied "Is it the wish of the Assembly?"; and when this question was put to the vote, a majority of only seven voted not to receive her Petition.

No doubt the Assembly was in an awkward situation having just, as they thought, disposed of the matter and then being faced with a second Petitioner. Nonetheless they were, in my opinion, neither courteous nor skilful in so putting Margaret Allan on the spot as they did. It was, I think, important that she brought her Petition supported as it was by a Petition signed by 909 pupils at Boroughmuir School where she was teaching. This also was intimated by the Clerk and duly recorded in the Minutes. Her case was no different from mine, and it was unfortunate that she should have been asked to show that it was. The significance of it was that she and I were in virtually the same position, so perhaps it was not just one eccentric individual who was deluded into thinking she was called to the Ministry.

Typical of a number of letters I received following the Assembly was one from the Rev Ian Mactaggart of Mayfield South Church in Edinburgh. He wrote, "I would like to say how very much I regret what happened on the last day of the General Assembly, and how much I, in common with a number of other sympathetic commissioners, am to blame. We were foxed and befuddled by the technical muddle, not least when the minister of the High Church (St Giles') appeared to use a technical breach of church law in order to prevent discussion even on the substance of the Supplementary Report. Will you please accept my apology for my share in the debacle?". Others wrote of their 'shame' and 'distress' at what had happened. But some saw signs of hope: to quote Ian Mactaggart again, "I find that the muddle has been providential and that many who had hitherto been neutral are now more sympathetic. I would not be surprised to see big changes even within the next year".

As usual, the fullest press coverage was in *The Glasgow Herald*, whose Church Correspondent wrote: "Confusion and frustration yesterday forenoon combined to make an extraordinary and humiliating mix-up of the particular petitions of Miss Mary Lusk and Miss Margaret Allan, and of the attempt to deal efficiently with the general principle of the ordination of women to the ministry. To everyone's bewilderment it emerged that, had the crave of the petitions been granted, it would have been impossible, under standing orders, to carry through the procedures essential to sending them down to Presbyteries under the Barrier Act; but had they come up on any day but the last no such technical problems need have arisen. That such an impasse should have meant an issue of such great importance petering out in technical chaos did not reflect well on those who direct the Assembly's business".

These were not my words, though I would have accepted them as a fair reflection of the wholly inadequate way in which the Church had so far faced up to, or rather failed to face up to, the question which I was laying before them. In the event, however, I was really now concerned not with the 'technical chaos', nor whether procedural points might have been used as delaying tactics, but rather with the fact that the Assembly had agreed to send the Panel on Doctrine's Report to Presbyteries. I had tried to express my dissatisfaction with it and, in the debate, the Rev Robert Gray, asking "Did the man Jesus not reflect a perfect image of God?" had stated mildly "We are open to a certain degree of heresy with reference to Theological Consideration No 5". Many people had expressed themselves mystified by this extraordinary re-writing of the Biblical doctrine of creation. And yet, this was what the Supreme Court saw fit to 'receive' and to send to Presbyteries for comment. The

Report was pilloried in the correspondence columns of *The Glasgow Herald* by the Rev Dr R W Stewart for its "mass of verbal acrobatics and speculative ingenuities". But by now it was too late: the Assembly seemed to have been bemused by the "fatuous verbiage" and instead of giving some kind of intelligible guidelines to Presbyteries it left them to make what they could of this extraordinary document.

However, the Clerk to the Presbytery of Glasgow, the Rev Andrew Herron, was not prepared to concede that there was any technical tangle in the Assembly and wrote to *Life and Work* in July in defence of the Assembly's procedure. He maintained that my "Petition was bound to be dismissed. It was incompetent, superfluous or irrelevant, and any of these faults was bound to prove fatal to it". His defence of these three possibilities I found unconvincing since the Assembly had in 1963 on the advice of the Procurator received the Petition as 'competent' and presumably also as relevant and not superfluous. Andrew Herron concluded his article with the paragraph: "For the sake of the record let me make it clear that I am not opposed to women being admitted to the ministry but I am bitterly hostile to legal short-cuts and to constitutional legerdemain. If the Church is now ready to admit women to its ministry, let us open the front door to them — not have one of them climbing in through a window".

I found this last phrase offensive, since it seemed to imply that I was attempting to get into the ministry by devious means, whereas I had taken great care always to act within the constitutional framework of Church law and procedure. I wrote a letter to *Life and Work* to that effect and received from Andrew Herron a generous apology: "I would assure you that no effect was intended and that in so far as anything I wrote conveys criticism of your actions or motives it is unreservedly withdrawn and my sincere apology is offered". When I wrote accepting his withdrawal and apology, he wrote again conceding that the phrase 'climbing in through a window' was unfortunate in that it did seem to put the initiative with me, which was not what he intended.

It may seem to the reader otiose to quote this exchange of letters both public and private since much of it rested on a misunderstanding for which apology was made and accepted. I do so for two reasons.

The first is that it illustrates the fact that it was very difficult not to become over-sensitive to criticism, especially from those who might be termed 'Establishment' figures in the Church. In this case the very imagery used of 'inside' and 'outside' was significant: the Clerk to the Presbytery of Glasgow was patently inside and I was outside, and although he did *not* think I was trying to climb in surreptitiously, nonetheless the picture remained; and being on the outside I was, of course, in no position to enter *on equal terms* into the legal argument, even though I could perhaps engage in theological discussion. This feeling of being an outsider because I am a woman has remained with me over the years. I am not sure that I am quite free of it yet — so powerful is the male dominance in the Church.

The second reason is that as well as mine there was another letter in the August *Life and Work*, and that was "An Answer to the Rev Andrew Herron by the Rev Frederick Levison". He made a number of points: (i) far from being superfluous in 1963, the Petition was essential for without it there would have been no action; it seemed that no one was willing to "open the front door" until someone knocked; (ii) the procedural difficulties reflected no credit on the knowledgeable people like Mr Herron who, being "not opposed to women being admitted to the ministry" should have sought to be helpful to Mr Bailey; and (iii) the Assembly failed in not providing an opportunity to discuss the case on its merits, as the majority who voted for the suspension of Standing Orders clearly desired, and in not following up the cogent criticisms made of the Report: puzzling over the question why those who found the Report

91

confused and theologically dubious did not move its rejection, he could only conclude that they thought this might lead to further 'remitting back'.

Maybe these points so cogently put encouraged me to think the following year that Fred would be a good partner to have!

*　*　*　*　*

In Chapter IV I have already recounted how I left the appointment of Assistant Chaplain at Edinburgh University and travelled to Ghana and India during the winter of 1964/65. As I had said to the General Assembly, my relinquishing of this appointment did not, in my view, invalidate my Petition because I should still be available wherever God might call me. In the meantime a call to the ministry could not be ratified; Presbyteries had to express their opinions and report back to the Panel on Doctrine.

Before recording the outcome of the debates in Presbyteries, I should perhaps write of two minor developments in the situation.

On 13 December the Very Rev Nevile Davidson, minister of Glasgow Cathedral and a former Moderator of the General Assembly, preached a sermon at the evening service "against the desirability of having women in the ministry". He maintained that "the demand" for women's admission to the ministry was "completely lacking" in the Church at large; he could find no scriptural evidence to justify their ordination; and such a radical departure from the age-old tradition of the Church "might create a new obstacle to reunion". It was this last point that made the headlines the following morning in *The Scotsman*. "Women in Kirk might be obstacle to reunion." I quote this as an example of two unconscious and unfair weapons used against us by some influential ministers: the first is similar to what we have already noted — the minister of Glasgow Cathedral was an 'insider' and could, if he chose, get headlines in the daily press by using his pulpit to speak his mind. The second is that by using the old argument that ordained women might be an obstacle to re-union, he put me and others on the wrong side of the ecumenical debate: we should have to carry the blame for the problem. Dr Davidson was a good friend. We had worked together on Inter-Church Relations matters, and I am sure he *intended* no hurt. I do believe that such men of influence did not realise the kind of power they wielded.

The other factor in the situation that winter was this. I was in India and out of touch with events at home and I was uncertain whether it would be wise or not to press my Petition further in any way at the 1965 Assembly. So I wrote to Dr J S Stewart, who was good enough to consult with the powers-that-be at '121' (121 George Street, the Church of Scotland offices) and after consultation replied that they thought it best that I do nothing. He wrote further that he believed the whole climate of thought throughout the Church had radically changed in the last two years and that the achievement of the main aim of my Petition was really coming within sight.

This was encouraging, because reports of Presbytery votes in November and December 1964 seemed to be pretty much divided on the issue. This was confirmed when the Panel on Doctrine presented their report to the following Assembly. On the question of the admission of women to the eldership, there was a clear majority of Presbyteries in favour; as a result the General Assembly agreed the principle, sent an Overture down to Presbyteries under Barrier Act procedure, and the Act was passed in 1966.

In the case of the ministry, of those Presbyteries which had taken a vote (and they had not been required to do so), nineteen had voted in favour and eighteen against. So the Panel's Report said that it seemed clear to them that "more time should be allowed to the Church to clarify its mind on this matter" and they asked to be allowed to prepare a further report on the theological issues involved, which they would hope to present the following year. Dr Sanderson, with characteristic frankness, told the Assembly that twenty years earlier he had been against women in the eldership. "I now see my mistake." He then declared "I want to see women in the ministry", but to this end he urged slow and deliberate action — a process of dialogue in the Panel and Presbyteries.

In the ensuing debate the Rev Robert Arthur proposed that the Assembly should declare that women are eligible for the ministry, and should instruct the Procurator and the Clerk to draft an Overture to go down to Presbyteries under the Barrier Act. On this occasion such a course would have been technically possible — it was not the last day of the Assembly. But caution prevailed and the Assembly resolved: "The General Assembly learns with interest" of the Panel's intention to prepare a further Report in the light of comments by Presbyteries on the theological issues involved in the admission of women to the ministry.

As my great supporter, the leader-writer in *The Glasgow Herald*, noted, my request for ordination made two years before had still "not been taken up". But we were all beginning to learn to be patient.

Shafts of hope came sometimes from the most unlikely quarters. That summer I met Dr Radhakrishnan, philosopher-President of India, and of course a Hindu. The Duke and Duchess of Hamilton kindly invited me to dinner at the Palace of Holyroodhouse where they were entertaining him on behalf of the Queen. Dr Radhakrishnan had clearly been told of my Petition and, when I was introduced to him, he asked me about it. When I said that I was not sure whether it would ever be granted, he replied at once: "Do not your Scriptures say, 'Ask and it shall be given you; seek, and you shall find; knock, and it shall be opened unto you'?". Of course; how could I ever have doubted?

The following week I was in the City of London, in one of the two pulpits in St Mary-le-Bow, engaging in a lunchtime dialogue with the Rev Joseph McCulloch, a popular Rector who was keen that the large audience of City workers should hear about what was going on within the Church of Scotland. Then on to the Annual General Meeting of the Society for the Ministry of Women in the Church (interdenominational) where my address naturally enough was given an enthusiastic reception. There were not many such opportunities to share our experience south of the border, though I remember later on being invited to preach in Great St Mary's, Cambridge; and on another occasion spending a day in Manchester at the invitation of the Bishop, Patrick Rodger, a Scot, discussing with the clergy of the diocese, at a time when the issue was due to come to the General Synod.

In September 1965 I was married to Fred Levison, then minister of St Bernard's-Davidson Church in the Stockbridge area of Edinburgh. I had got to know Fred while I was teaching at St Colm's because there was a close connection between the College and St Bernard's-Davidson, where students and staff shared in Sunday School and youth work. I had been leader of the 14-18 age group, normally called a Bible Class: we called it the Square Circle and used informal methods of learning (which at that time were less common), such as debates, drama, role-play, quizzes, visual aids and new songs and hymns. It was a lively group, one of the brightest of the youngsters being Martin O'Neill, now a leading Labour politician. My connection with the congregation broke off in 1961 when I left St Colm's. Fred's wife, Eleanor, sadly died of cancer at Christmas 1963. In April 1965, shortly after my return from India, Fred and I became engaged.

Our engagement was received with much goodwill and friends hoped that soon we would be able to have a joint ministry. But not everyone saw it that way. When Fred met Professor J H S Burleigh, the distinguished church historian and Moderator of the General Assembly in 1960, he was congratulated most warmly on having removed the Church's problem at a stroke! Professor Burleigh assumed that both I myself and the question of women's ordination were now dead ducks. A doctor in Nagpur, India, received a letter from a minister at home saying "We think Fred Levison should be given a DD because he is removing Mary Lusk from the field.". Professor J K S Reid thought half the problem was now out of the way: he said to the Assembly in 1965, "While the original petitioner, as members of the General Assembly will no doubt know, has moved to an altered status, the General Assembly, through the Petition, has to decide upon the issues to which the original Petition gave rise". This caused me to write to *The Scotsman* saying that I was not sure what Professor Reid meant, but that I thought it must be that he assumed that my forthcoming marriage altered my ecclesiastical status in such a way as to render my petition for ordination no longer applicable. I went on to say that should the Church decide to open the ordained ministry to women, I would assume that there could be no question of imposing a condition of celibacy on such women as were called and ordained.

Actually this issue had been raised at various points in the long discussion, but never explicitly tackled. Long before, in 1926, one of the speakers in the then Assembly of the United Free Church of Scotland, speaking against the admission of women to the ministry, said "It would mean the introduction of a celibate order into the Church": he seemed to regard that as axiomatic. In more recent discussions the question of marriage had been raised as presenting practical difficulties: "What would happen when a woman minister was married and wanted to have children?". This never seemed to me to be a question for the Church to answer; it was rather a question which an ordained woman would have to work out for herself, as was the case in every other walk of life. This is certainly what has happened.

The concern about marriage and motherhood being incompatible with the parish ministry had a number of aspects. It was partly concern for the young woman herself. Assuming that once married a woman's first priority should always be to the home and family, the question was asked "How could she possibly cope with both that and the calls of a parish?" It was also concern for the parish. "Let's face it," said one eminent churchman, "the duties of a parish minister involve being on call for 24 hours out of 24, and seven days a week", and he did not see how a young mother could always be available when the parish needed her.

But there also surfaced a deep-seated taboo about pregnancy. "Minister objects to pregnant ministers" was the head line of a press article recording discussion in one Presbytery where a member had said "We are not so desperate that we need women ministers. The prospect of a woman six months pregnant preaching in the pulpit is not an edifying one". Even in Advent, one might ask, when the whole Church is expectant?

The question has also been raised whether there should be special dispensations for women in the ministry. Maybe there should be. Maybe the Church has been slow to recognise that a woman's pattern of life is different from a man's, and that this may require new patterns of ministry: some may want to serve part-time, and some may want to take a number of years off to have and to rear a family. But what has in fact happened is that parish ministers have worked it out their own way with the support and encouragement of their husbands and congregations. Perhaps in time a PhD thesis may evaluate the benefits and disadvantages of the ministry of mothers.

So far as my immediate situation was concerned, I was a deaconess. Hitherto, deaconesses had resigned on marriage, but no objection was raised to my desire to remain a deaconess. And so it was that married deaconesses were simply accepted in the church. Now there is a large proportion of them, just as there are married deacons. However, in 1965 when the Swedish President of the international Diakonia wanted to propose me as his successor, he changed his mind on hearing of my engagement, not because he had any difficulty with the idea of a married deaconess, but because the German Motherhouses would not find it acceptable. I continued to enjoy good personal relations with them, but not as President.

*　*　*　*　*

1966 can be reported on quite briefly. The Report of the Panel on Doctrine was released on 17 May. In the section headed "The Place of Women in the Church" the Panel explained that the study which they had hoped to complete within the year had taken longer, "and all the Panel can do at present is to report diligence". They had set up a working party, which included a number of new members, and which was being assisted by biblical and rabbinic scholars. They hoped to be in a position to report the results of this study to the General Assembly next year.

In response to an invitation from the then Editor, Denis Duncan, I wrote a short article which appeared on the front page of the *British Weekly* of 19 May. Quoting the four consecutive years in which a report to "the next General Assembly" had been promised, I asked: "How much longer do we have to chase the mirage of 'next year's Assembly' before the General Assembly itself is to be allowed to act in this matter as what it claims to be — the supreme court of the Church?". I pointed out that the biblical work had been done by scholars all over the world, and that the Panel itself had given us a bibliography of some fifty titles in their 1964 Report. And I complained that so far the Church had made no move to test what I believed to be my call. Once again *The Glasgow Herald* spoke out: it quoted my article quite extensively and in yet another leader suggested that it was high time for the Church of Scotland to come to a decision.

The same rather restive mood was reflected in the Assembly when it took up the matter on Wednesday June 1. The new Convener of the Panel on Doctrine, the Rev John Heron, was somewhat defensive in his account of the progress of the Panel's work and, indeed, of their function. "As the Panel sees its task, it is not for it to make authoritative pronouncements on matters of doctrine. Only the Courts of the Church can do that."

Very well then, let the Assembly pronounce. But no, that was not to be. The Rev Duncan Forrester of Madras protested that if one of his students after a year's hard labour produced such a remarkably uninformative essay as the Panel had given the Assembly, he would find it hard to commend him for 'diligence'. The question was simple, and had not yet been answered: whether a woman can be freely called by God to the Ministry of Word and Sacraments. The Assembly should be allowed to give a reply to that question.

A strong attempt was made by the Rev George Nicholson (who had retired to Argyll from ministering in the USA) to get the Assembly to take the matter out of the hands of the Panel on Doctrine and get a decision forthwith. Saying that the basic issue was one of human freedom — the liberty of a woman in Christ to be and to serve in any capacity whatsoever, Mr Nicholson went on: "I maintain that the issue before this General Assembly today — before this Panel at any rate — is no longer a matter for a Panel on Doctrine; it is a self-evident proposition of the liberty of the Gospel, which is our Reformed inheritance". There must be a response to the petitions. He wanted the Assembly to take the necessary steps to promote legislation. But — would you believe it? — this could not be done. Once again this was the last day of the Assembly. The only way would have been to instruct the General Administration Committee to bring an Overture to the next Assembly.

So the Assembly was faced with the choice of releasing the Panel from further responsibility and taking the matter into their own hands, or agreeing to wait another year for their further Report. In an unguarded moment Mr Heron said, "Nothing would please me personally more than to have nothing more to do with this matter". But the Assembly decided not to let him off the hook. The Panel was left to pursue their Biblical study with no specific instruction, but only an undertaking from the Convener that they would do their best to report next year. There was no doubt that many in the Assembly were frustrated and impatient: it appeared that the Panel was not prepared to make an authoritative pronouncement, nor was the Assembly itself in a position to meet the challenge of the original petition and reply to it.

Those of us who were 'waiting in the wings' had no way of knowing where the Panel's biblical study would lead and what conclusion they would lay before the Assembly in 1967. Lest it should be inconclusive or advocate further delay, six of us thought that we should ourselves prepare a statement urging the Assembly to come to a decision. We agreed to do this in the form of "An Open Letter to the General Assembly of the Church of Scotland" which was released to the press after publication of the Panel's Report. It read as follows:

This appeal comes from six women who believe that they have been called to the Ministry of Word and Sacraments, and that the time has come for the Church of Scotland to take a decision on this question.

We believe that the theological principle at issue is quite simply the following: that God can and does call women to the ordained ministry of His church.

We do not intend to argue the theological case here: that has been done many times before, and there would appear to be an increasing consensus of opinion in the churches that there is no valid theological reason against the admission of women to the ministry.

If that is so, then we venture to suggest that the General Assembly of the Church of Scotland should not delay further by merely sending the Report of the Panel on Doctrine to presbyteries 'for their information'. Rather, the General Assembly itself should initiate action now, for the following reasons:

a) The present situation in which the Church of Scotland both ordains women to the eldership and licenses women to preach the Word, but refuses to ordain women to the Ministry of Word and Sacraments, is clearly anomalous.

b) Within the Presbyterian tradition an increasing number of churches admit women to the ministry; twenty-two member churches of the World Alliance of Reformed Churches now ordain women.

c) In the meantime, candidates are being lost to the Church of Scotland. At least eight women members of the Church of Scotland have become ministers of other churches; there are at the moment a number of women in the theological colleges, and it is not known how many others may be called.

d) The question of the relation between the Church of Scotland and other denominations must not be allowed to obscure the issue. If the Church of Scotland is persuaded that the theological case is sound she should act, possibly in consultation with churches with whom she is already in conversation. Further, is not action necessary in order to avoid the anomalous situation described in the proposed Plan of Union with the Congregational Union of Scotland?

e) If the Church of Scotland were to reach a positive decision on this issue, then not only would individual candidates be available to her ministry, but we believe that a new freedom might be experienced at all levels of the Church's life, and new patterns of ministry be worked out by men and women in partnership.

We beg the General Assembly to face the basic question — submitted in a Petition in 1963, referred to the Panel on Doctrine for consideration but not answered in their reports — viz. the reality of God's call of a woman to the ministry. If we are in error, show us our error. But if our belief is sound, then we ask that the Church should take steps to remove the barrier, in order that the call may be tested of any woman who may present herself to the Church as a candidate for the ministry.

Claude Barbour, Ministère Feminin, Certificat
    d'Etudes Religieuses
Margaret Forrester, MA, BD, DCS
Elizabeth Hewat, MA, BD, PhD, DD
Mary Levison, BA, BD, DCS
Mary Weir, BA, BD
Sheila White, MA, BD, DCS

We sent a copy of the Open Letter to Mr Heron as a courtesy, and we asked permission to circulate it to all members of the Assembly. This was not granted by the General Administration Committee on the ground that whatever is circulated "may be regarded as an official document". However, the press coverage was considerable. We called a press conference in the Edinburgh YWCA, which was well-attended, and we got a sympathetic hearing when we said that our hope was that some member of the Assembly would press for a decision, as we were not in a position to do so ourselves. *The Scotsman* and the *British Weekly* reproduced our letter in full, and other papers gave the main points; so that Commissioners to the forthcoming

Assembly could hardly fail to hear what we were trying to say.

From their own reading of the Report, the press had already discovered that the Panel was divided. The Vice-Convener, the Rev Alex Sawyer, was quoted as saying "We've tried to be fair and impartial so that no one could say we were trying to influence the General Assembly". I must admit I find that strange: I do not recall any other issue on which the Panel has thought it their duty to be so detached and impartial. But the point seems to have been that they were quite unable to reconcile different views of the authority and interpretation of Scripture among their own members. So having set out the New Testament evidence with exegetical comments, the Report then proceeds to give two conflicting theological positions, View A and View B, and to present both these with equal weight to the Assembly. The Panel hoped that the Assembly would receive the Report "as fulfilling the remit given to it in 1960, and instruct that it be sent to the Presbyteries for their information". This would presumably have meant the acceptance by the whole Church of the impasse which the Panel had reached: no action would have ensued.

The New Testament study was undertaken by a Working Party under the chairmanship of Dr Alan Galloway of Glasgow University. Curiously, they did not appear to have looked at the Gospels, but confined themselves to passages in St Paul's letters and the Pastoral Epistles. This means that, apart from Galatians 3:27, ("In Christ there is neither male nor female"), they were examining texts concerned with marriage and with the practice of the New Testament Church with regard to the activities of women in worship and the limitations imposed on them. The Panel was very honest in its admission of the difficulty of knowing how to interpret these passages. As Dr Galloway told the Assembly, "We have each to decide" which of the criteria set out in the Westminster Confession with regard to the interpretation of Scripture applies, *either* "what is clearly and decisively set down in Scripture" *or* where the worship and government of the Church "are to be ordered by the light of nature and Christian prudence, according to the general rules of the Word, which are always to be observed." Therefore if this somewhat subjective decision is taken, different conclusions are reached. View A — that the passages examined offer no guidance to the Church of today; View B that they are normative for all time. View A concludes that there is no bar to the admission of women to the ordained ministry: View B that there is.

The Report came before the Assembly on Tuesday 23 May — not the last day; and once again the Rev W Grahame Bailey was a member and had a motion down on the Order Paper. These were two hopeful omens.

Grahame Bailey exhorted the Assembly to make a break with tradition and to end the present absurd segregation in the Church: "Take down the barriers, and the Church will be immeasurably enriched". His motion was that the Principal Clerk and the Procurator should be instructed to draft an Overture to be sent down under the Barrier Act enabling women to be ordained, and to submit it to a later session. Seconding the motion the Rev Robin Barbour, a noted New Testament scholar, said of the Westminster Confession criteria that *both* the light of Scripture *and* the light of nature and Christian prudence were leading in the direction of the proposed Overture. He questioned whether the authority of the male could be asserted in this age, suggesting that in the new creation the proper relation of men and women was rather co-operation. No longer could the Church make a hard and fast distinction between a presbyteral ministry for men and a diaconal ministry for women.

Possibly the most influential speech was that of another New Testament scholar, the Very Rev Professor James Stewart. Paying a warm tribute to the honesty of the Panel on Doctrine, Professor Stewart said it was clear that setting one text against another would never solve the question. He went on, "It will be tragically ironic if we create a new legalism on the basis of the writings of St Paul, who was the greatest anti-legalist of them all". If Paul were to hear some of our debates he would surely say "The letter killeth, but the Word giveth life". The whole letter to the Galatians, not just 3:27, is "the trumpet call of evangelical religion in every age, the charter of the Free". Finally, he reminded the Assembly that Paul's own call did not come through any Church channels: "never again can we question a claim to have received the call of God through a non-traditional channel of the Church".

The vote was decisive: 397 for Grahame Bailey's motion, and 268 against. The proposed draft Overture was submitted to the Assembly on Saturday 17 May, when the Assembly duly accepted it. This meant that the Panel's Report was sent to Presbyteries for their information, and the draft legislation was sent to them for a vote, Yes or No. This was very much in line with what our Open Letter had hoped: a decision would now be taken one way or the other.

* * * * *

Any readers who have followed me thus far through the labyrinthine ways of the decision-making processes of the Church of Scotland will be glad to know that the end is in sight.

Presbyteries up and down the land debated the issue in the autumn. According to reports, those opposed to the proposal seem to have laid more stress on practical difficulties, such as marriage and motherhood, than on biblical arguments, except in the Highlands and Islands, where some Presbyteries were unanimously opposed on biblical grounds. But the great majority of the votes were in favour, especially in the cities: Edinburgh 170 for, 48 against; Glasgow 236 to 143; Aberdeen 89 to 31, though Dundee was equally divided. The final figures overall were: Presbyteries approving 42, disapproving 17, equal vote 2. The individual votes of members of Presbyteries, which also have to be recorded, were: approval 1,817, disapproval 1,030. The majority of Presbyteries being in favour meant that the 1968 Assembly would be able, if so minded, to pass the necessary legislation, though they would not be obliged to do so. And the substantial size of the adverse vote would no doubt be used as an argument against decisive action.

That was, in fact, just what happened. When the Presbytery votes were reported to the Assembly on Wednesday 22 May 1968 and the appropriate Committee recommended that the Assembly "adopt the Overture and convert the same into a Standing Law of the Church", there were attempts to propose a direct negative and to refer the question to kirk sessions and congregations for their consideration. However, neither of these proposals received significant support and in about 35 minutes the vote was taken. It was such a clear majority in favour of the legislation that it was not even necessary to take a count. It now became the Law of the Church that: "Women shall be eligible for ordination to the Holy Ministry of Word and Sacraments on the same terms and conditions as are at present applicable to men". Announcing the decision, the Moderator, The Rt Rev James Longmuir, said "We have certainly made history in the Church of Scotland today".

VII — Frustrations

No, I was not the first woman to be ordained in the Church of Scotland. I have made that disclaimer times without number since 1968. The first was another deaconess, Miss Catherine McConnachie, BD, assistant at St George's, Tillydrone, Aberdeen. She was ordained by the Presbytery of Aberdeen on 27 March 1969, thereby earning her place in the history books. That was as it should be: she was already a fairly senior deaconess working in a parish, qualified and ready for ordination. At the time I was not in an appointment, and not looking for a charge apart from my husband's. I had no ambition to be 'the first', and was greatly relieved not to be subjected to all the publicity which would have surrounded that. My time would no doubt come.

Meantime, I do have to confess to a great sense of achievement when the legislation was finally passed and all offices in the Church were now open to women. I was happy to receive congratulations from friends, from the late Lady Stansgate and the English Society for the Ministry of Women in the Church of which she was President, and from *The Glasgow Herald*, who yet again devoted their first leader to the topic:

> "The General Assembly is to be congratulated on the magnificent majority by which it yesterday agreed to admit women to the ministry of the Church of Scotland. It took courage to break a tradition stretching back more than 400 years, but it was a just and honourable decision and the logical consequence of admitting women elders two years ago. The Church of Scotland has always been a strongly masculine institution . . ."

I have to admit to a glow of pride when the article goes on

107

to suggest that my "dignity, intelligence and restraint" may have helped to convince many traditionalists, and to bracket my pioneering role with that of Sophia Jex-Blake in medicine and Nancy Astor in parliament.

I should like to take up the word 'restraint' in this article, and to say how important I thought this to be. During the five years 1963-68, and for long afterwards, the language used to describe what I was trying to do distressed me. People spoke of my "battle" or "campaign" or "fight" with the Church: they thought that I was heading a protest movement for women's rights. But it was not in fact like that at all. It will be evident from what I have already written that what I was concerned to say to the Church was simply that I believed myself called to the ministry and that I wanted the authorities to examine this call in the light of the gospel of grace. There was no orchestrated campaign: I suppose the nearest we got to that would be the 1967 Open Letter signed by six of us who shared this conviction. I conscientiously declined all invitations to take part in anything that could be construed as 'lobbying', and it may be worth placing on record some of the numerous approaches which I received.

I turned down a proposal that I should write in the journal of the World Alliance of Reformed Churches. I likewise refused to write a chapter in a projected paperback to be published by the Society for the Ministry of Women in the Church, and I declined their invitation to speak at their Annual General Meeting in 1964, finally succumbing in 1965 when my actual Petition was no longer *sub judice* but had been dismissed. Even then I was reluctant to become involved nearer home in anything resembling a campaign. I declined to serve on a panel of speakers on the subject of the ordination of women being drawn up to address, when invited, secular women's organisations. And I quite explicitly left to other interested people such proposals as the revival of an organisation called The Fellowship of Equal

Service, or the establishment of a Scottish Branch of the Society for the Ministry of Women in the Church, or any educational campaign within the Church.

Perhaps I was over-sensitive on this issue, but I did not want to leave the slightest loophole for the kind of remark referred to earlier by the Clerk of Glasgow Presbytery that, the door being shut, I was attempting to climb in through a window. I was aware that neither the General Assembly nor Presbyteries like to be 'lobbied' from outside: the fact that I and my colleagues were inevitably outside would still not have justified any attempt to sway the opinion of the insiders. Even since the winning of the argument in 1968, I have always held aloof from groups, committees and organisations promoting the right of women to greater equality of participation in the Church. My reluctance has sometimes been misunderstood by other women, but I have thought, rightly or wrongly, that my role is a rather different one — as a woman to serve as best I may and let others draw conclusions. The only time when I have ever joined a 'women's lobby' was in 1988 when I was asked to speak for a group concerned that there should be adequate representation of women on the new ecumenical bodies being set up in Scotland. I rather think that then we were able to gain a sympathetic hearing precisely because I was known *not* to be a part of any pressure group. It has been important to me that this should be so, and that the whole debate should have been as little adversarial as possible. That we have achieved what we have without giving offence and with a minimum of conflict is a matter for satisfaction. Wrestling there has been, but that is surely a different thing from fighting and campaigning.

* * * * *

I have now to pick up my own story at the point of my marriage in 1965.

Fred Levison was one of the family of three sons and one daughter of Sir Leon and Lady Levison. His mother was English and his father Jewish and a convert from Judaism — hence the name Levison. Leon's father was an eminent rabbi in Safed, one of the holy cities of Palestine. Leon was destined to look after the family vineyards, but he came under the influence of a Scottish mission, read the New Testament and was convinced that Jesus was the Messiah. He had to leave home and family, and so travelled to Scotland in 1900. Fred, in his retirement, wrote the story of his father's early struggles, his long service with the Edinburgh Jewish Mission, his secret service work in the Middle East in the First World War, his widespread travels on behalf of the International Hebrew Christian Alliance of which he was President, and his heart-breaking efforts to rescue Hebrew Christians from Hitler's Germany. He died in 1936. *Christian and Jew* was the title of Fred's book, because his father always maintained that he was Jewish by race and Christian by grace and, far from being incompatible, the second was the fulfilment of the first.

In his youth and working life Fred was completely thirled to the Church of Scotland; and it was really only in later years of comparative leisure that he came to ponder on his Jewish background and heritage. As a mere Scot, I have always found this intriguing and I encouraged him to write. One of the most fascinating holidays which we had together was in Israel in 1972, when we met over forty of Fred's relatives.

Fred has encouraged and helped me all along the road. I recognise in him so many of the gifts of the Spirit in which I know myself to be deficient; and we are in many ways complementary to each other, making for a happy and fruitful partnership.

Fred is twelve years older than I am. By 1965 he had

110

already been a minister for twenty-eight years. After ten years (interrupted by war service as a chaplain) in his first parish at St Andrew's Church, Coupar Angus, he and Eleanor (Fred's first wife) moved to Edinburgh to St Bernard's-Davidson Church. When we were married in 1965, their eldest daughter Ann was already married, and Elspeth and Freda were still at school. It was hard for them to have their father marry again, and there were adjustments to be made on all sides. Nevertheless, we soon became very good friends, and in the course of time I have been very happy to be adopted by all their families as an honorary granny. Having been already eighteen years in St Bernard's-Davidson where he had had a very full and happy ministry with Eleanor at his side, Fred was now ready for a move. But that did not prove to be very easy to achieve.

During the three years that we remained in Edinburgh, apart from the new duties of family and being a minister's wife in St Bernard's-Davidson Church, I was greatly involved in the planning and carrying through of the International Conference of Diakonia (the World Federation of Deaconess Associations) in Edinburgh in 1966. Up to that time the Federation had always held their conferences on the continent of Europe and the setting had been Deaconess Motherhouses with their large resources and traditions of hospitality. We thought it important that deaconesses of the Motherhouse pattern should experience something of our parish-based system, but we had to start from scratch with very limited resources so far as conference premises and organisation were concerned. Led by Dorothy Gardner, our inspired and indefatigable President, the whole Deaconess Council became involved in the three years 1963-66 in praying, in planning, in making financial contributions. We invited all the Deaconess organisations in the United Kingdom to meet with us at Dunblane to share in the planning: this was in fact the first time we had met together — a fruitful spin-off from the international conference.

When the time came, we had a marvellously successful and enjoyable conference based in University halls of residence and meeting places, and worshipping in historic Edinburgh churches — St Giles' Cathedral, the Kirk of the Greyfriars and the old Charteris Memorial Church (now Kirk o'Field) with its associations with early deaconess work and training. I had the enormous privilege of preaching the sermon in Charteris Memorial, when I took for my text Luke 12:37: "Blessed are those servants whom the master finds awake when he comes; truly, I say to you, he will gird himself and have them sit at table, and he will come and serve them". I wanted these selfless servants of their fellows to ponder on the marvel of themselves being served by the Master.

The whole conference helped, I think, to enhance the fellowship among deaconesses of different traditions and many lands. It undoubtedly also gave to us in Scotland a renewed sense of our participation in the worldwide Church.

The question arose of becoming an office-bearer in the World Federation: this could not be President because of my marriage, as I have already explained. The post of Secretary was vacant and my name suggested, but I felt that that would not be the right way for me to go since it would divert my energies too much away from the Church of Scotland to the satisfaction, no doubt, of those who would have been happy to see this awkward customer going elsewhere.

At home it remained quite hard to gain acceptance and doors were evidently not going to open of themselves. Fred was a member of two Clubs — one, the Clerical Club, was clearly a club for ministers only; the other was the Theological Club which would not seem to be restricted by its title to ministers or to men. However, when Fred asked the Theological Club if, in view of my theological training and interest, I might be invited to join, the answer was a firm negative. The Rev Rudolf Ehrlich, a Leith minister and theologian of repute, said "If she comes, I go". He was noted for his bluntness, but there were others too who declared that they would leave the club. We were entirely mystified by this attitude: was the club devoted to maleness as much as to theology? Fred stayed with them, though he felt like leaving when he discovered that not one of his friends in the club was willing to make the smallest move to open the door to a woman even in this entirely unofficial setting.

The more important problem facing us however was to find some sphere of ministry in which there would be need and room for both of us together. Fred applied for several vacant charges, only one of which heard him preach. In our innocence we thought that congregations would be interested in what we had to offer — two for the price of one. On the contrary, we discovered that they were suspicious of this "deaconess licensed to preach" and were afraid she would not fit in to their conception of the role of the minister's wife. Another vacancy committee invited us both to an interview, and although I left the talking to Fred he apparently (so we heard much later) used the pronoun 'we' too often, as in "We would make youth work a priority". They felt they would be safer with a bachelor! It appeared that as an over-qualified wife I was, in fact, a hindrance.

Fred was finally called to Greenlaw, a small Berwickshire town whose Kirk Session and congregation, though conservative in almost everything, were willing to accept me in whatever role we saw as appropriate. This meant that for the nine years we were there I was able not only to lead in such spheres as the Woman's Guild, the Bible Class, training of Sunday School teachers and Christian Aid; I also shared in the conduct of Sunday worship and preaching. In fact in a culture where all leadership is left to 'incomers', this was welcomed. Not being fully stretched by Church and home, I tried to serve the community. I became Secretary of the newly-formed Community Council, and for several years dealt with trees and pavements, rights of way, bus shelters and similar matters, endeavouring to articulate the community's wishes in dealings with local government and other authorities. Greenlaw was a somewhat introverted community, and I did what I could to bring to the village some interesting people: George Foulkes, later an MP, to the Woman's Guild; Dr Herrick Bunney of St Giles' Cathedral for a recital on our renovated organ; and Geoff Shaw, by then Convener of Strathclyde Regional Council, who preached at our Festival Service one summer.

Beyond the parish I was able to do a certain amount of pulpit supply work, mainly at the invitation of old New College friends — Bob Henderson in Melrose and Joe Brown at Yetholm. Other opportunities came my way, though not many, it must be said, from ministers in our own Presbytery who seemed to prefer to send to Edinburgh for holiday supply. In fact, the Presbytery of Duns itself, although supposed to take note of any deaconess 'within the bounds' and invite them annually to one of their meetings, virtually ignored me. Except for my co-option on to the Overseas Committee, whose convener was an enterprising layman, the Presbytery did not seem to think I had anything to offer.

When the chaplaincy at a small geriatric hospital became vacant on the departure of the minister of Gordon, Fred was asked by the Presbytery to take it on. He responded with the suggestion that I might look after the old people, doing all the chaplain's duties except the twice-yearly Communion service which he could provide. The response of the Presbytery was to appoint a young minister who lived eighteen miles away and had just taken on a triple linkage.

Eventually in 1973 an opportunity for an ordained ministry arose, only to vanish again in what seemed to be Presbytery red tape. On the retiral of the minister of Eccles, a hamlet five miles away, I was invited to take several services during the vacancy. When the Presbytery decided that Eccles should be linked with Greenlaw, Fred and I discussed with the Session Clerk of Eccles the possibility of my looking after Eccles within such a linkage if the Presbytery were willing to ordain me. I would be willing to give full-time service, or as much time as was required, asking for no stipend and requiring no manse. The Session Clerk was enthusiastic about the idea, which he was sure would be acceptable to the people of Eccles. However, the Presbytery would not consider it, and added Eccles to what was already a triple linkage served by one minister. They were evidently anxious not to set a precedent, meaning, we supposed, not to let Greenlaw-Eccles have two ministers when this would be reduced to one on our departure. (But then a younger minister would have come and taken on both.) When a couple of years later Eccles was again unlinked and again Fred was asked to take it on, we were wise to the situation. He agreed and became minister of the linked charge; we shared the services in the two churches and I did much of the pastoral work at Eccles.

Things might have worked out differently now, when it has become more accepted that ministerial couples should offer for various forms of joint ministry; although even yet not all the problems inherent in that have been solved. Nevertheless, in our time at Greenlaw it was already possible for women to be ordained: I was fully qualified and willing and not necessarily looking for any remuneration. Alternatively, I was available, without ordination, as a deaconess licensed to preach; but there seemed no great eagerness to use me. Would any other organisation, I have often wondered, be still in existence if it were so wasteful of its resources in personnel as the Church has sometimes seemed to be?

One of the reasons why so often the Church of Scotland is unable to use people is that they do not fit in to the categories of eligibility for Courts or Committees laid down by the Church. Many years later, on a visit to the General

Synod of the Church of England, I was struck by the widely representative nature of that body. It may well be open to criticism on other grounds, but its representative nature is far ahead of our Courts. It is able to call on the whole resources of the Church, since the only criterion of eligibility is membership of the electoral roll. In consequence, the Church of England is able to use the very considerable experience and expertise of top people in business, politics and other spheres, who in our system would scarcely have time to give to the eldership with all that that entails. At the other end of the spectrum, there were in the General Synod young lay men and women and clergy wives, whose voices are seldom heard in our Courts. Moreover, for most of my working life, women have been very under-used on the Committees of the Church. Before we became eligible in the sixties for the eldership and the ministry, there was a category of 'women members', but these were always in a small minority and not appointed as Conveners and Secretaries. Even now when there is no sex barrier women are only gradually percolating through the system and have yet to achieve anything like a proportionate place in the decision-making processes. I have to say that I have only recently felt free to make a natural and useful contribution in these still predominantly male structures.

However, in our Greenlaw years, there were two spheres in which I was able to make some contribution in the wider Church: one was the ecumenical Scottish Churches' Council, and the other was the Deaconess Council. It has to be said that, in the eyes of the Church of Scotland, both were marginalised and powerless and therefore areas in which women could operate. It was a fact that long before women gained acceptance as decision-makers in our own Church, we were able to take full part in ecumenical councils. The Church of Scotland was willing to appoint representatives, men and women, ministers and lay people, presumably in the knowledge that they had no power to commit the Church to anything: power remained with the Church's own Courts. To me as a woman the whole ethos and feel of ecumenical councils was different: there was a ready acceptance of one's contribution for what it was worth and not for who one was, which was liberating to those of us who were no one in particular.

As I recounted in Chapter IV, I had already worked with Dr Robert Mackie on the Scottish Faith and Order Conference at St Andrews in 1963. I later became a Church of Scotland representative on the Scottish Churches' Council, and Convener, from 1968-72, of one of its key committees, the Committee on Local Co-operation and Mission. We were active in the promotion of local ecumenism throughout Scotland, and organised annual conferences at Scottish Churches' House, Dunblane, for representatives of local Councils of Churches. We worked closely with the Secretary of the Council, the Rev Andrew Wylie, who did a marvellous job for the council, travelling tirelessly the length and breadth of the country. Lack of response from so many who did not want to be disturbed in their set ways led to considerable frustration and illness for Andrew, leaving our Committee very much in the driving-seat. We did our best to keep the show on the road, and this meant for me endless trips from Greenlaw to Dunblane. But it was satisfying that through our efforts and those of others the Scottish Churches' Council was able to survive a difficult period.

In 1974 I was elected President of the Deaconess Council. Although I was not technically in an appointment, the Deaconess Board were good enough to recognise me as being on the Active List of Deaconesses on the strength of my various activities, and I was therefore eligible for office. To be elected by one's colleagues is always a privilege and honour, but in this case I was particularly delighted: my deaconess colleagues might well have thought that I was by now somewhat out on a limb, more of a minister-in-waiting than a deaconess-licensed-to-preach. However, then and later, I have always found a warmth of acceptance among them, and I was very happy to serve as President for three years.

The seventies were a frustrating time for deaconesses so far as our position in the church was concerned. It was during that time that the term 'diaconate' emerged in the thinking and documents of the Church, and deaconesses were asserting that they were not to be regarded as a 'women's ministry', but as a distinctive office complementary to the ministry of Word and Sacraments. This had been recognised in the 1962 Scheme for Deaconesses, i.e. the regulations approved by the General Assembly. But there was a realisation both in the Deaconess Board and among deaconesses themselves that we had not yet reached satisfactory solutions to a number of problems. Why were there so few in this office, and why was the Church at large not more aware of them? Why were there no men? What was the right relation of deaconesses to the Courts of the Church? There were large issues involved in the question of the integration of the diaconate in a Reformed Church with its long-established system of Courts composed of ministers and elders.

The Deaconess Board in conjunction with the Home Board (the main employing body) were very active in these years through a joint policy working-party (on which I served) and in repeated attempts to make proposals to the General Assembly. But although the Assembly in 1972 welcomed the proposal for a diaconate of both men and women, when it came to working out and presenting the details of what was envisaged, the Board was again and again unable to carry the Assembly with them. Perhaps our thinking had not yet sufficiently matured: almost certainly the Church as a whole was not yet receptive to new thinking in this area. Nevertheless, inch by inch, advances were made, and when we come to consider (in chapter IX) the steps that it was possible to take in the eighties, we shall see that seeds were sown in the sixties and seventies which made these advances possible.

In the meantime, of course, deaconesses continued to give really self-sacrificial service to the Church, mainly in areas of social deprivation; some did not question their lot, but others were frustrated by unhappy (or non-existent) team work, by lack of consultation and exclusion from decision-making processes both in the parish and in the wider Church. The Council, meeting twice a year, was not only a very open and enjoyable fellowship; it was also a forum for the sharing of problems and difficulties. It was important that we had this channel through which our views could be fed in to the ongoing process of policy-making; and it came to be more and more accepted that deaconesses themselves had a contribution to make to discussions which in previous decades had been conducted by others on our behalf and often in a rather patronising way.

To be President of the Council and, by virtue of that, Vice-Convener of the Deaconess Board was therefore a pivotal position, in which I was very much aware of the trust placed in me by my colleagues and did my best to justify that trust. Those three years provided a good and fulfilling task at the end of the Greenlaw period.

* * * * *

After the Eccles fiasco, we remained at Greenlaw for only eighteen months after which Fred retired at the age of 67. In the ordinary course of events he might have continued to the statutory limit of 70; but we thought that if he were to retire there would be a better chance of my finding an opportunity for an ordained ministry. We returned to Edinburgh in September 1977, but four months later he was invited to become the *locum tenens* for a few months at the Scots Kirk in Rome. This was an opportunity too good to be missed:

we exercised a joint ministry in preaching and leading worship in this excitingly cosmopolitan congregation. It was during our time in Rome that plans were laid for the appointment which was at last to lead to my ordination.

VIII — Ordination

The Parish Church of St Andrew and St George in George Street, Edinburgh, stands at the heart of the commercial and retailing centre of Edinburgh. Built in 1784, the first church in the Georgian New Town, it has a comparatively small number of residents in the parish; but there is a vast number of workers in banks, insurance companies, building societies, hotels, shops and stores and other businesses in its vicinity. The Rev Andrew Wylie, minister of the charge and, of course, a friend from Scottish Churches' Council days, was working out his vision of outreach into the parish — of the 'gathered' congregation putting themselves at the service of the working population. This involved two-way traffic: an invitation to all to come into the Church and Undercroft, open every working day for lunches, with opportunities for worship and pastoral care; and in the other direction, ministers going out into the workplaces of the parish as agents of the Church with the message and the caring which the Church could be expected to offer to men and women in their daily environment.

The ministry to shops and offices was pioneered by Andrew Wylie and by Dr Robert Mathers, a senior minister of great experience who was the Associate Minister. When Dr Mathers was due to retire in 1978, the Presbytery gave approval for the appointment of a successor who would be not under 55 years of age and would be designated Assistant Minister. (The reason for demoting the post from Associate to Assistant is not entirely clear. As Assistant Minister I was frequently asked when I was going to move to better myself!) The post was advertised while we were in Rome; on our return I submitted an application, was short-listed, 'heard' and interviewed. I was appointed by the Kirk Session at the end of July (1978), to start work on September 1.

The letter of appointment stipulated that the appointment was offered "on the understanding that you will secure ordination within a reasonable time". That was however not a simple matter. What was required in order to achieve it was that the procedures which were normally spread over a number of years, three or four at the least, should be telescoped into a few months. Nearly thirty years before I had, I suppose, started along the wrong road — the only road then open to me; and although I was fully qualified and had years of experience behind me, the authorities nonetheless had to get me through a whole series of hoops before I could be ordained. I had to (i) be nominated by the Presbytery as a candidate for the ministry; (ii) apply for and pass a Selection School; (iii) undertake (or be exempted from) Bible Examinations and practical training; (iv) get an Exit Certificate; (v) undergo Trials for Licence; (vi) be licensed as a probationer; and (vii) serve (or be exempted from) a probationary period. Only then would ordination be possible.

Both the Presbytery of Edinburgh and the Committee on Education for the Ministry did their best to be accommodating to this quite involuntarily awkward customer. I was nominated as a candidate; passed Selection School; was not required to undertake the Bible Examinations and practical training laid down by the Church; was granted an Exit Certificate; and was exempted from the probationary period. We had a bit of an argument over licensing. As a deaconess I had already been taken on trials for licence and "licensed as a Preacher of the Word", in accordance with the Act of Assembly of 1956. I was anxious that this authorisation under which I had been conducting worship and preaching for twenty-one years should not be called into question, as it would have been had the process been repeated. The rub was that I was not a probationer for the ministry (see page 38), and only probationers can be ordained. In the event, the Presbytery agreed not to require of me 'Trials for Licence', but to license me as a probationer for the holy ministry at an ordinary meeting of the Presbytery. This they did on November 7; and although I think no one was quite sure what was happening, honour was satisfied and I became ordainable. (The Moderator of Presbytery told me that, since he knew I did not want to be re-licensed, he had found an ancient formulary which would make me an Expectant — not perhaps the happiest of phrases!)

The whole process began in June, when I sent in my application schedule, and was completed by November 30 when I was ordained, three months after starting in the appointment. Five and a half months is probably some kind of a record, but I am not sure what. From another perspective, however, it could be said that the process had begun in 1963 when I petitioned the General Assembly. Fifteen years had been a long wait, and when the moment finally came it was marvellous to find myself surrounded and encouraged by family and friends who had waited and watched with me all those years. Many who had helped me in 1963 were there in 1978, and this meant much to me.

It was St Andrew's Day, and the Church of St Andrew and St George was well-filled. I was supported by Fred on one side and Bob Mathers on the other; Andrew Wylie led the service and preached with his usual loving warmth. The Presbytery of Edinburgh ordained me. We lifted the roof with our praises — so much so that the organist in her enthusiasm managed to fuse the organ and all the lights and the last hymn had to be sung to the piano in candlelight! It was Isaac Watts' great hymn of praise — one of my favourites:

> *Join all the glorious names*
> *Of wisdom, love and power*

with its last verse:

> *Now let my soul arise*
> *And tread the tempter down:*
> *My Captain leads me forth*
> *To conquest and a crown:*
> *A feeble saint shall win the day*
> *Though death and hell obstruct the way.*

It had not quite been "death and hell". But this feeble saint did feel that not a few obstructions had been overcome, and that she was now being led forth into a new and fulfilling phase of ministry. This is not to say that I belittled what had gone before — my ministry as a deaconess: on the contrary I gloried in it. But so long as the ordained ministry was denied to me and to all my sex, the wrestling had to be carried through to its fulfilment. "I will not let you go unless you bless me" was what I had presumed to say to the Church all those years ago: now at last, after much wrestling and praying, she blessed me and sent me forth.

* * * * *

I worked for five years in the fascinating appointment of assistant minister and chaplain to the retail trade in the parish. The parish minister was himself developing the church's outreach into the commercial sector. My remit was to maintain and expand the work in the shops and stores; in addition, I was responsible for the pastoral oversight of the aged and "shut-ins" within the congregation. It was made clear that I had complete responsibility in these two areas of work, while I also shared in the leadership of worship on Sundays and weekdays and in the general life of the congregation.

I spent at least four mornings a week in the stores — John

Lewis, Jenners, C & A, British Home Stores, Martin and Frost and other smaller shops. The large stores were visited every week, and for them all it was important that the chaplain's visit was paid regularly on a known day. This, among many other things, I learned from my predecessor Bob Mathers, who introduced me to this new behind-the-scenes world of large department stores. He had been very faithful in his visits and I tried to be the same, declining several invitations to serve on committees of the wider Church which would have taken me away from my stores.

The task as we saw it was to make oneself available as a minister to the many hundreds of people who worked in the shops and stores, not only in the selling areas but also in management corridors and coffee-rooms, in offices and stock-rooms, in kitchens and restaurants. Much of the time the contact was inevitably superficial, but by dint of endless "Good morning"'s and "How are you?"'s, one became 'a kent face' and a friend, so that when there was trouble of some kind a members of staff would open up to the chaplain and there would be opportunities to help. The Church was there at the invitation of management, and personnel managers and others were often willing to call on the chaplain in cases of sickness, bereavement or other such situations.

I was aware that I inherited the goodwill built up by Bob Mathers. With very rare exceptions I found a warm welcome, and I would say that — perhaps rather to our surprise — people were very grateful that the Church should take the trouble to come and spend time with them in their place of work. It is also very good for a minister to be meeting people on their own territory, where they are at ease, rather than expecting them always to cross the threshold of a church building and to learn our ways and language. So many people would never dream of coming into a church that if we are to be in touch with them we have to make ourselves available where they are.

There were other aspects of this outreach to the shops and

stores — carol services at Christmas, Bible Study groups, hospital visiting, baptisms, weddings and funerals. The chaplain had, of course, always to be aware that everyone lived in someone's parish and one of the small services one could provide was to put the shopworker in touch with her or his own parish minister. But with that minister's permission, there was sometimes good reason why a wedding or funeral, or less often a baptism, should be conducted by the chaplain. Home visits to shop staff who were, for one reason or another, off work took me all over the city and beyond in the afternoons, and I tried to dovetail these in with visits to the elderly of the congregation in their homes or in hospital.

It was good that the assistant minister had congregational responsibilities as well as the stores chaplaincy. St Andrew's and St George's rightly saw the work of outreach as involving the whole congregation. This meant staffing the Undercroft with volunteers to welcome people and to serve lunches; it meant supporting the work in prayer, and the 'shut-ins' had a prayer card to help them share in this; it meant participating in various events which brought together the Sunday and the weekday 'congregations'. From the chaplain's point of view it was very important not to be a freelance minister but to be the agent of the congregation whose home was the fine Georgian building with its splendid spire pointing to the heavens, symbol of the reality that, in the midst of all the getting and spending, there is another dimension to life; that, too, is what the presence of the chaplain in the workplace symbolises.

All this was, of course, not my vision, but that of Andrew Wylie who, throughout his ministry, has been marvellously effective in spurring the Church on to serve 'on the frontiers', the latest setting of his ministry being the oil industry. He has recently retired. Andrew was committed to the idea of team ministry, and we greatly enjoyed working together, discussing fresh ideas — more often his than mine

— on worship, on contacts with groups of people, on events, on ways of working and financing the whole enterprise and so much else. Under his leadership, St Andrew's and St George's, though small in numbers, was extrovert and enthusiastic and found a valuable role as a city centre congregation. It was a great privilege to be a part of it.

I was unfortunately off work through illness for several months in 1982-83. My appointment was for "five years in the first instance", and the five years expired on August 31 1983, when I should be over 60 and beginning to think of retirement. I indicated that I should, if it were helpful, be willing to continue for a further limited period, but the Kirk Session decided to make a new appointment for the next five years so that the outreach could be further developed. In consequence I retired at the end of August.

However, even in retirement I managed quite unwittingly to contravene the regulations. This distressed me because I really thought that by then my argument with the Church was a thing of the past. I was a woman of 60 and the normal retirement age for women is 60; in fact, deaconesses were required to retire at 60 and were not allowed to carry on in fulltime employment. I had been conditioned by that and it never occurred to me that my position might be otherwise; but I had not read the small print, so I had not appreciated that women who are ministers are treated by the Church as though they were men and therefore do not retire until 65.

In this situation I ran up against two snags. The first was that I did not qualify for a pension. It would in any case have been very small after only five years' service, but the trouble was that though I had worked for five years I had only been ordained for four years and nine months. There was therefore no way I could be paid a ministerial pension.

The second problem was that in all Church laws and regulations no distinction was made between women and men in the ministry — no doubt it would be argued rightly so — and this included the age of retirement. The question therefore was my status in regard, for example, to the Presbytery. I was at first told that I could not retain my seat in the Presbytery, because until I reached the age of 65 I was a "minister without charge" and not eligible for membership of Presbytery. However, after further correspondence, the Business Committee accepted that I had *in effect* 'retired' and the Presbytery agreed to grant me continuing membership.

One of the questions at issue here was the interpretation of the "Act anent Admission of Women to the Ministry" (1968), which said that women are eligible for ordination "on the same terms and conditions as are at present applicable to men". It did not seem to me to be self-evident that this implied that the Church should make no distinction *thereafter* between women and men. It had never entered my consciousness that on becoming a minister I should be regarded as any less a woman: hence, I suppose, my too facile assumption that normal practice which applied to women — for example on retirement — applied to me as well. Whether or not the Church should make particular provision for women in the ministry in this and other matters is, I think, a question yet to be tackled.

My own feelings were somewhat ambivalent. I should have been happy to give another two or three years to St Andrew's and St George's, but that was not to be. It would scarcely have been realistic to seek a call to a charge at the age of 60. The only way to have served further would probably have been to look for another appointment as an Associate Minister or some such position. In the event, my health being not too robust, I was glad to accept retirement, and continuing membership of Presbytery and of various Committees including the Assembly Council, a key committee of the General Assembly. I became Convener of the Council's Committee on Planning and Priorities, and was able to give quite a significant amount of time to that very interesting work. Two years later, when Andrew Wylie left St Andrew's and St George's and the charge became vacant, I was minister *locum tenens* in the ten-month vacancy. Later I was able to give three months as *locum* at St Colm's Church.

All this added up to six years' service spread over a period of nine years. This was not much as the Church regards the ordained ministry; and I was never a parish minister. It might have been different had I been born thirty years later or had I known myself called at twenty rather than at forty, or had I not married a minister, or . . . But the way things did in fact work out was, I believe, the way of God's guiding. It might well be asked, was it all worth it — all the struggling to have my call recognised and then so long to wait and so few years of active ministry? The answer most certainly is "Yes"; not only for the satisfaction of my own brief ministry, but far more because it opened the way for others. One of the great joys of these later years has been that for a generation now, young women have been able to enter the ministry quite unaware of the struggles of the earlier years.

★   ★   ★   ★   ★

The number of women in the ministry of the Church of Scotland has grown gradually over the years. So far as I am aware, the Church as a whole has found this to be an enrichment of her ministry and has had no regrets about the decision taken in 1968. It is true that there is still difficulty with the whole concept to be found in some quarters, including some vacancy committees appointed to find new ministers for charges; with the consequence that women sometimes have difficulty in finding a charge. There is, I think, a quite common fear of the unknown, and in a situation in which, in the nature of things, most congregations have no experience of a woman ministering, they are wary of entering into unexplored territory. But I have not heard of any congregation which, having called a woman, has been dissatisfied with her ministry on the grounds of her being a woman. It is also true that there are as yet few, if any, women in what might be regarded as the prestigious charges, just as there are few women conveners of the major committees of the Assembly. I rather think that this is due not so much to prejudice against women but rather to the fact that it is taking time for women to work their way through the system. There are women with wide experience in other spheres now in the ministry, but there cannot yet be many with long experience of the parish ministry.

Of the six women who wrote an Open Letter to the General Assembly in 1967, three of us have in the event served in the ministry of the Church of Scotland. (Of the others, one is now deceased, and two are in ministry in North America.) The Rev Sheila Spence (née White) was ordained in 1979 and has been a parish minister since then. The Rev Margaret Forrester's contribution to the Church of Scotland would in itself justify the decision to admit women to the ministry. Margaret, having graduated MA, BD from Edinburgh, became a deaconess licensed to preach, and then was married and went to India with her husband Duncan, who was teaching at Madras Christian College. I stayed with them briefly in 1965. Margaret sought ordination in the Church of South India, but the Bishop of the diocese, Lesslie Newbigin, although not averse to the ordination of women in principle, thought he should not ordain one who had come from a Church which as yet did not ordain women. Furthermore, he quite understandably believed that the first woman to be ordained in that Church should be an Indian — as was, in fact, later to be the case. The Forresters returned to England on Duncan's appointment to the University of Sussex, and Margaret was able to be ordained in the United Reformed Church in 1974, and to minister to a small congregation. Some years later they were back in Edinburgh where Margaret served first as Assistant Minister at St George's West, and then took on the challenge of St Michael's, a struggling congregation which was allowed to appoint a minister only on a five-year terminable basis. Under Margaret's leadership the congregation came to life again. Membership increased by over a hundred in two years, and the charge was restored to full status. The demands of the charge became such that she had to relinquish the chaplaincy of a Technical College in order to cope with it all. As well as her evident success in the parish, Margaret gives valuable service in the wider Church, and in particular has won the respect of the Assembly's Board of World Mission and Unity, of which she is currently Convener.

If I single out Margaret Forrester from among those women who are in the ministry of the Church of Scotland, it is because she and I have travelled much of the road together. But one could equally well point to the acceptable and fruitful ministries of dozens of women up and down the country. Some are married, some single; some are mothers, some are not; each one has been able to work out her pattern of ministry according to her own circumstances. The Church should not expect a consistently perfect performance from women any more than she does from men. But equally, I think, no cause has been given for a verdict that women have fallen below the standard required.

The question is sometimes raised as to whether a woman is a different kind of minister from a man. Do we think and speak, worship and work differently because we belong to different sexes? Does the presence of women in the ministry alter the character of the ministry itself? If so far it has not, will it in the future? And should it?

In the 1960s, when the question of ordaining women was before the Church, questions were also being asked about the nature of the ministry and the meaning of ordination.

131

Some said that we cannot ordain women until we are clearer in our own minds what it is we are doing when we ordain someone to the ministry (though this did not prevent the continued ordination of men). Others said that to ordain women would in itself be a change in the structure of the ministry which might lead to other needed changes. An interdenominational consultation at Scottish Churches' House, Dunblane, in 1967 suggested that the Church must understand the world in which she is set, and recover a conception of the ministry of the whole people of God to that world; only in that context could she determine what kind of ordained ministry is needed for the building up of the whole body. Such discussion has continued over the years without, I think, any steps of great significance being taken. There have been developments in the provision of community-ministries and team ministries; there has been the rather ambiguous institution of the auxiliary (non-stipendiary) ministry; and the position of the diaconate has been strengthened. But the basic pattern of the parish ministry remains the same: the presence of women does not appear to have been an influence for change, either disruptive or progressive, according to your point of view.

The fact is that the ministry as a collective body is still very much a man's world. "Why can't a woman be more like a man?" Professor Higgins' question in *My Fair Lady* reveals the unspoken assumption behind some men's attitudes — and some women's too — wherever women enter any hitherto male preserve. Those of us who came into the ministry in the comparatively early days were concerned that we should slot in unobtrusively to the pattern already established, while at the same time not becoming "more like a man". Perhaps if there comes to be a more even balance in numbers and influence between women and men, there may be changes in style and structure. In the meantime, although there have been one or two casualties — women who have found the system so uncongenial that they have dropped out, for example — change can only evolve gradually as men and women become accustomed to working with each other in the ministry.

Again, when there is a small number of women in any largely male profession or organisation, the question arises whether the women have, or want, any special support system, either officially or unofficially. There is a certain ambivalence among women on this matter. On the one hand, we do not want any form of positive discrimination or preferential treatment, but simply to be accepted on merit. (Curiously, when men were admitted to the hitherto female diaconate — see next chapter — it was put to me that we ought to see to it that they were given ready access to positions of leadership.) We are not a special category of 'women ministers', and the use of that title, which is fairly common, should be countered by the phrase 'men ministers'. But on the other hand, it is not easy, unless one sets out to be aggressive, to be a woman in a man's world, and there may well be felt a need for mutual support and encouragement.

I am interested to find that in the Divinity Faculty of Edinburgh University (New College) where there is now quite a substantial number of women students, they have a large and flourishing Women's Forum. In a recent number of the *New College Bulletin* a member of the Forum writes: "It has provided an oasis of support in the midst of an environment where, although a good proportion of students now are women, there remains a strong sense of a male tradition . . . We can mull over lectures and discuss issues that affect us as women. But most important of all, we can bask in the knowledge that we will not be drowned out, interrupted or criticised. We can quite simply, be".

Those of us who have gone on into the ministry find ourselves in a far smaller minority. Although we may be expected to have greater experience in handling relationships, there is no shame in an admission that we might welcome the occasional company and support of our female colleagues. From time to time we have, in fact, had an informal gathering of women who are ministers in the Church of Scotland, or rather of those who were interested in such a gathering. Some reacted strongly against any such invitation, asserting vehemently that as ministers they were in no different situation from their male colleagues. But others have been glad to talk about such matters as perceived discrimination and the difficulty in getting a call; a feeling of powerlessness; the isolation of those who through family circumstances are for a time not working; and the possibilities of job-sharing. Women, especially married women, have a different pattern of life from men; and it may be that if our gifts are to be fully used by the Church, she has to find ways of accommodating us rather more flexibly.

One area in which the Church has begun to adapt to the presence of married women in the ministry is that of opportunities for ministerial married couples, of whom there is a growing number. It is now possible for a husband and wife, both of whom are ministers, to serve together in a parish on a job-share basis: that is to say that a Presbytery may induct them jointly to a single charge. Joint and shared appointments, whether each is part-time with a clearly defined division of duties, or full-time where there is need for two ministers, are recognised by the Church as appropriate for married ministerial couples. In practice this may not yet be widely appreciated, and there are such couples who have not been able to find joint or shared employment. But the practical issues involved were addressed by the Assembly Council in a very sensitive and forward-looking report to the General Assembly in 1991. The whole tenor of this report is positive and helpful: it suggests to the Church that there is here a new and distinctive resource available to her, and that steps should be taken to match this resource to parishes which could appropriately be served by ministerial married couples.

There is also the recognition that such couples may want to meet and share experiences, thereby benefitting from a mutual support system. The Assembly, in accepting the Council's recommendations, took a positive step forward in what I see as the step-by-step assimilation of married women into the ministry and the adaptation of the traditional pattern to accommodate them and use their gifts.

I find it hard to answer the question whether a woman is a different kind of minister from a man, i.e. whether we actually do the job differently. On this I am content to be agnostic and to let others judge. When I was chaplain to the shops and stores, where the great majority of employees are themselves women, they used sometimes to say that they appreciated having a woman as chaplain. But I do not attach any particular significance to that since they have equally gratefully accepted the ministries of my male predecessor and successors. I suspect that women in the parish ministry find the same sort of response and attach as little importance to it. We all — men and women — have different gifts, and I am not at all sure that individual gifts can be attributed to one sex or the other. What matters is that we should be free to be ourselves and offer what we can.

I do not like the term "woman's (or women's) ministry" — a phrase used more often in Anglican circles than in ours. If it is purely descriptive of ministry performed by women, then that is all right. But if it is an attempt to define something, then we should be wary of it; if it refers to a ministry different from that of men, then question it, because this will almost certainly mean an inferior ministry prescribed by men for women. When we reach the point, as we have now in the Church of Scotland, that any ministry may be exercised by either a man or a women, then the term 'women's ministry' becomes both unnecessary and confusing.

★　★　★　★　★

135

This is not the place to discuss at any length the importance of feminist theology, even if I were qualified to do so. But I should perhaps make a few comments — random and inadequate as they may be — on the bearing of feminism on the issue treated here of a woman's calling to the ministry.

The charge has been made against the Church of Scotland that the decision to ordain women was grounded not in theology but in feminism. "The campaign for women's ordination originated not in divine revelation but in modern feminism and that has led to fatal confusion in the Church". These are the words of the Rev Donald Macleod, writing in *The Scotsman* in June 1991. He is a minister of the Free Church of Scotland but is respected in all the churches as a voice of the 'evangelicals'. I would rebut strongly the allegation that my plea for the recognition of my calling was not founded in the Word of God: as I have attempted to set out, I believe that what is at issue is nothing less than the gospel itself and that the freedom which the gospel has granted to us all in Christ demands that a woman's calling be recognised.

But what is interesting is Mr Macleod's assumption that it is improper for the Church to pay any heed to modern feminism, which he accuses of leading to 'fatal confusion' in the Church. Feminism has a bad name for its strident speech and aggressive stance: women trying to make themselves heard in male-dominated contexts almost inevitably raise their voices and become combative in tone. I understand this only too well and have always tried to avoid it and it is unfortunate that feminism so often carries these overtones.

Properly understood, both feminism and "the women's movement", which is the more broadly-based concern for women's freedom in the modern world, are unexceptionable. Feminism, according to the dictionary, is the "advocacy of the claims of women"; and a feminist is a "supporter of women's claims to be given rights equal to those of men". This I would accept and therefore I am happy to be called a feminist. If I were to attempt a definition of Christian feminism, I should leave out all references to 'claims' and 'equal rights', which have no place in a Christian stance, and I should say something like this: Christian feminism is the recognition that the gospel of Christ demands that the Church acknowledge women to be fully capable of receiving the grace and calling of Christ; there can be no sex-related disqualification. I am a Christian feminist.

I do not claim to be a feminist theologian, probably because I was born too soon: there was little word of feminist theology when I learned my theology. Further, I am unhappy with the protesting character of some feminist theology which arises out of hurt and is, understandably, liable to be characterised by anger. Nevertheless, feminist theology should be carefully listened to by male theologians and churchmen as a sign that all is not well — that women feel excluded and angered by the assertion of male superiority. This must be taken seriously. Feminist theology is a clear warning signal that the Church has to make room for the participation of women at all levels, as the New Testament church appears to have done before the position of women was gradually eroded by a male assertion of superiority.

Of course, women have an important contribution to make to the study of theology (which is a different thing from being feminist theologians). In the nature of things, and largely unconsciously, we come to this study from a rather different perspective: we have a different feel for what a human being is. We may well, therefore, have new insights to bring to biblical studies and to the formulation of Christian doctrines. I owe to Dr Daphne Hampson (*Theology and Feminism*, Blackwell, 1990) the illuminating suggestion that women may well conceive of sin and salvation in different terms from men, since women have been prone to the undervaluing of themselves rather than to pride, and we may see salvation in terms of healing and the restoration of self-worth rather than of the breaking down of self-centredness (pp 116-131).

If women can be set free from sexist discrimination, then we shall, without hurt or hostility, be able to contribute to the human (not exclusively male) activity of talking about God. There is need, for the sake of the health of the Church, that our contribution should be freely made in theology, in ecclesiology, in liturgy. It is claimed, for example, for the St Hilda Community — a radical feminist group of women and men in London — that there is a distinctively feminist character in the informality of their worship and in the absence of any priestly hierarchy. The banishing of any sense of denominational division is also said to be a feminist achievement. This escape from the rigid (male-conceived) structures of the Church is given the credit for a new vitality and enthusiasm. That may well be. The important thing is that they find that they have 'space' to worship naturally and freely. They may start as a protest movement arising from a feeling of being excluded, but such a group may also have important things to say to the Church.

One of the problems faced by feminists, both women and men, in the Church is the use of masculine language and imagery with regard to humankind and to God. For myself, I have over the years not needed inclusive language. I belong to a generation which always assumed we were included in such biblical language as, for example, "sons of God" in the Beatitudes and in Paul's writings. But the problem is that once the question is raised and one becomes conscious of the masculine language then one may feel excluded, and I do recognise that the present generation have been in this way 'conscientised' and so do feel excluded. The Church has therefore now to adopt inclusive language and be careful always to speak of human beings rather than men (which is of course made more awkward by the fact that the English language has only one word for man).

The language used of God has also been largely masculine

138

in gender. That does not imply sexuality in God. The growing tendency to use the word 'gender', which properly applies to nouns (words), to apply to people confuses the issue. In my view, the use of a noun of masculine gender, eg chairman, for a position which I may hold says nothing about my sex: it does not attempt to make me male; it is simply a masculine word. By the same token, I do not take the Christian imagery — masculine though it may be — to be exclusive of me as a woman. I have always assumed that the incarnate Christ took my flesh as well as that of any man. But the fact is that many women of a younger, more self-aware generation now say this is not possible. Again, the Church has to hear the feminist cry and seek ways of formulating, or re- stating that God is beyond all sexual attributes and that the maleness of Jesus is secondary to His humanity.

One last comment on Donald Macleod's denigration of modern feminism (page 137) is this: I do believe that feminism, the movement for the freedom of women in society as a whole, is of the Spirit. The Church is inclined to look for the working of the Holy Spirit exclusively within her own confines, but the biblical witness is that God may also be at work beyond the bounds of Israel or of the Church. In the case of feminism, the Church has, in fact, lagged behind the movement in society at large; but that movement actually bears witness to what is basically a corollary of the gospel. The Church should not be ashamed to admit this and to learn from these secular evidences of the Spirit's working. It may be only in the new-found self-awareness of women, due to the secular movement for emancipation, that we are now able to hear God's call to ministry. But that does not mean that it is any the less God's call, originating in His Word.

IX — The Diaconate Again

The 1970s were a time of painfully slow growth so far as the recognition and standing of deaconesses were concerned. The Report of the Deaconess Board in 1972 had suggested that the Church recognise a diaconate for both men and women "as being an integral part of the total ministry of the church and having a distinctive role within that ministry". But five years later the Board perceived that "several lines of thinking in the Church now seem to be converging on the establishment of a diaconate, and we await the maturing of this thinking. The Board is eager for the full recognition of deaconesses as deacons of the Church, but is waiting for the church to be ready for this move forward". The following year this was put to the test in the Assembly, but the proposal was referred back, mainly because the term 'diaconal agent', used in the Report as a noun of common gender, did not find favour. ('Deacon' was said by some to be pre-empted by Deacons' Courts, which was why 'diaconal agent' was suggested.)

But that same 1978 Report set out clearly the new perspective from which the Church was now able to view the diaconate. "Although it is now ten years since the Ministry of Word and Sacraments was opened to women, it has taken time for the full implications of this to be grasped. Now we have come to see that the opening of all offices of ministry to women as to men means that there is now no distinction of eligibility with regard to gender for any office of ministry. *All nouns used to describe the holder of any office in the Church can be assumed to be of common gender*. The term 'deacon' and the term 'deaconess' are interchangeable. Therefore it is necessary to present once again the doctrine of the diaconate in the knowledge that where historically distinctions were made between men's and women's service this is no longer so for the Church of Scotland. We are not talking of women's ministry: we are talking of a form of the Church's ministry. For the first time in the history of the Church the man/woman dichotomy can be disregarded in this respect. What the New Testament says of 'deacon' applies to the 'deaconess' in the Church of Scotland in 1978: what the 'deaconess' of the Church of Scotland of today incarnates is a manifestation of the historic diaconate."

I would regard this as itself an historic statement giving expression to what we had struggled towards for so long. The 1968 Act made this demolition of the sex-barrier possible, and finally in 1979 the consequence for the diaconate was realised when the General Assembly recognised "the office of the diaconate" to be open to both women and men. This was a landmark in the evolution of what had been up to this point the deaconess movement relegated to the margins of the Church, now emerging into the mainstream of the 'official' ministry. A Celebration and Thanksgiving was held in November in Cluny Church, Edinburgh, the service being conducted by Dr Roy Sanderson who had been involved in so many ways with this evolution in ministries over the last quarter of a century, and the sermon was preached by Professor Tom Torrance. When, as Moderator, Professor Torrance visited the Deaconess Council in 1976, he had delivered a lengthy and typically erudite address on the ministry of the diaconate, in which he developed the thesis that the diaconal ministry is "the service of response to the Word", complementary to the presbyteral ministry which is "the service of the Word". Deacons act as representatives of the people and as examples of the way in which Christ identified Himself with their need, and therefore examples also of pure unassuming service, in which the whole people should engage in response to the Word of God. This theme he took up again in his sermon to the newly recognised diaconate.

Although 1979 was a landmark — from now on we speak of

the Diaconate Council and the Diaconate Board — it has to be said that it did not bear fruit for another nine years: there were no male recruits to this hitherto female ministry.

In the meantime, the Panel on Doctrine was given a remit by the General Assembly in 1982 to clarify the Church's theology of ministry and the relation of the various ministries one to another. This did not in the first instance produce any great clarification so far as the diaconate was concerned; but after further consideration and consultation, the Panel's final Report in 1989 included a strong statement on the ministry of the diaconate. Not only did this Report give a fair description of the service of the diaconate; the Panel also recommended that they should be given greater resources and a higher profile, and that they should have a recognised place in the Courts of the Church. But that is to anticipate.

For twenty years there was one hand in particular on the tiller of diaconate affairs which should certainly be acknowledged. Kay Ramsay was a parish deaconess who had been a journalist and who managed to combine her work in the parish with the duties of Secretary of the Deaconess Board from 1963 to 1980, when she became for three years President of the Council and Vice-Convener of the Board. Kay is a great servant of the Church: she has brought to bear on diaconate questions deep spiritual insight and clear vision coupled with an undaunted patience and persistence. Hers has been a very steadying influence, and her gift of writing has been invaluable in giving expression to what many have thought and felt. For Kay, as for so many deaconesses, the horizons of her ministry have always been as wide as the whole World Church: this, too, has greatly enriched diaconate thinking.

* * * * *

For eight years I was myself out of touch with diaconate affairs. On my ordination in 1978 I ceased to be a deaconess, and although I still felt myself to be very much one of them, I had no reason to take part in Councils and local groups. In 1986 I was invited to be Convener of the Diaconate Committee. My immediate reaction, which I expressed in my first letter to deaconesses was that it was high time we had a deaconess as convener; but that was technically not possible while deaconesses still had no place in Church Courts. Failing that, I accepted gladly, since I still knew what it was to be a deaconess; and my four years as convener gave me, in my retirement, very satisfying opportunities of being of some further service to the Church.

It was an exciting time to come back. After a few quiet years we were on the verge of celebrating the centenary of deaconesses and perhaps also of seeing a number of long hoped-for advances come to fruition. We had, I think, an unprecedentedly full and busy four years in the Council and the Committee. What we were able to achieve was due in no small measure to the caring and imaginative leadership of the Council Presidents, Jean Morrison and Margaret Cameron; to the loyalty and hard work of Joyce Nicol and Kate Jameson in the office; and later the herculean efforts of Yvonne Teague who took over single-handed the manifold tasks of Secretary. It was a great joy — and great fun — to work with them and many others.

It would be neither appropriate nor possible to cover all our concerns here, although I am aware that what I omit may in the event turn out to have greater significance than some of what I include. For example, the question of pastoral support for the diaconate; in-service training for teams; the widening of the scope of service beyond the parish, and the commissioning of candidates directly to that service; the possible development of a non-stipendiary diaconate; ecumenical and world-wide relations with diaconal groups; yet another re-organisation of committee structures in the Church of Scotland offices, putting the diaconate physically in the ministry corridor; the sanctioning by the Assembly of an increase in the strength of the diaconate. These were all important matters, and no doubt there were yet others. But I have chosen to write of five areas which I should want to be remembered as having been associated with the four years of my convenership. These are the Centenary celebrations and entering into the second century: the accession of men; the Scottish Ecumenical Encounter on the Diaconate; membership of Church Courts; and the new Commissioning Service.

* * * * *

The celebration of a centenary is an occasion for looking in three directions — back over the completed hundred years with gratitude for all that has been accomplished; inward to assess whether the present is faithful to the past and adequate as a spring-board for the future; and forward to attempt to discern the direction in which God is calling. The diaconate does not stand still; for as long as I can remember we have been on the move, challenging the Church to take us seriously and to give us an appropriate place from which to operate. In approaching 1988 therefore we were clear in our own minds that we should not expend too much time and energy thinking of the past, but rather attempt to "raise the profile" of the diaconate in the present and use the occasion as a launching-pad for forward moves.

I think we got the balance about right. We did look at our roots: each deaconess was given a beautiful illuminated scroll, designed by Val Duff (then deaconess at Wester Hailes, Edinburgh), signed by the Moderator of the General Assembly. This scroll recalled Phoebe the first *diakonos* of the Church (Romans 16:1) and Lady Grisell Baillie, the first deaconess of the Church of Scotland, set apart in 1888.

"Thus was the Order of Deaconesses restored in the Church of Scotland. One hundred years on, the Church celebrates 'Varieties of Gifts — Varieties of Service' given by Deaconesses, Church Sisters, Parish Sisters, all united in 1949, recognised as a distinctive office in the Church in 1962, an office opened to men in 1979." The name of the individual deaconess was inserted together with the place and date of her commissioning; in this way each was made aware of standing in the great succession.

Significantly these scrolls — of which I am very proud to have the original with my name inscribed on it — were presented on December 9 1988, the exact centenary of Lady Grisell Baillie's setting apart, at a Celebratory Meal and Communion Service held at Garthamlock and Craigend East Church, Porchester Street, Glasgow. Significantly, because Garthamlock is a deprived area in the East End where a deaconess was serving; this setting provided an instant reminder of the present reality. It was a marvellously happy occasion, on which I was greatly privileged to celebrate Holy Communion as we all sat, one family, round candle-lit supper tables.

We paid a visit back to Bowden Kirk and to Mellerstain House in the Borders, to recollect the story of Lady Grisell Baillie and to say prayers in the Kirk where she was set apart. But when it came to deciding what should be written and published in celebration of the centenary deaconesses were clear that it should be not a history but a Book of Prayers and Meditations for the present. *Windows of Prayer* is a beautiful collection of thoughts and prayers rooted in life as it is lived by deaconesses in their workplaces. Discerning the presence of God within what appear to be the most unlikely circumstances is a great gift, and this the diaconate shared with all of us in this little book. At New Year 1988, copies of *Windows of Prayers* were presented to the Deaconess Hospital in Edinburgh for the use of patients.

This was followed a few days later on January 8 by a

Celebration of Thanksgiving in Kirk o'Field Church next door to the Deaconess Hospital in the Pleasance. This is the former Charteris-Memorial Church, where we had worshipped on the occasion of the great World Deaconess Conference in 1966, and where once again we were reminded of our history by the very stones. With the help of visual aids we recalled the past, looked at the present, and outward to world-wide diakonia. Deaconesses from France and Zambia spoke; Sister Ute Hampel was President of the European area of the 'Diakonia', and our Zambian guest was Mrs Justina Vwalika, engaged in deaconess training at Kitwe and doing a year's study at St Colm's. Then the Word of God: the National Bible Society presented a Bible, from which a deaconess read and I preached. Finally the diaconate and then the congregation were invited to join in a prayer of re-commitment for the future.

This was a public service in which many friends and Church leaders shared, and we had good press coverage of it. We were concerned to get publicity not only for this great occasion but also for the normally unsung achievements of deaconesses. Thanks to *Life and Work* and to helpful guidance from Ann Davies, the Senior Press Officer of the Church of Scotland, some of the newsworthy stories began to surface in the local and national press.

The next national occasion was the special Centenary Council at Carberry Tower in May when we were honoured to have with us Deaconess Inga Bengtzon of Uppsala, Sweden, President of the World Federation of Diaconal Associations and Sisterhoods. She also addressed the General Assembly on May 23 on the occasion of the Centenary Report. In presenting that report, I had the enormous privilege of speaking to a packed House on behalf of deaconesses (who could not yet speak for themselves) to remind the Assembly of Dr Charteris' original vision of the revival of the New Testament diaconate and of the achievements of the first hundred years. The Assembly agreed with enthusiasm to "give thanks to God for one hundred years of service to the Church by Deaconesses, Church Sisters and Parish Sisters; acknowledge the valuable contribution made by gifted and committed women in a wide variety of spheres; and congratulate the present diaconate on their centenary, take note of the ways in which this centenary is being marked, and wish them well in this year and for the future". The step forward which we invited the Assembly to take was the recognition of lay missionaries as deacons, and to this we now turn.

★ ★ ★ ★ ★

As we noted in Chapter IV, although Dr Charteris' vision was the restoration of the New Testament diaconate, it was at the same time the opening up of an avenue of service for trained and committed women in particular. For many years the Order of Deaconesses (and the kindred Parish Sisters and Church Sisters) was the only avenue of trained service open to women in congregations and parishes, and it was therefore naturally regarded as a woman's ministry. Some of us, however, had never accepted that way of defining the diaconate, and the situation was definitively clarified in 1968 when the ordained ministry was opened to women. The office of deaconess could now no longer be defined as the ministry for women. In that year the Convener of the Home Board said, "We must have one diaconate, male and female". The Home Board in fact did nothing over the next twenty years to bring this into effect. In 1975 the Moderator of the General Assembly, Dr James Matheson, said "A diaconate of men and women, ordained, with their proper place in the Councils of the Church, is absolutely inevitable". But, as we have seen, it was not until 1979 that the Assembly resolved that "the office of the diaconate shall be open to both men and women", and that "the holders of the office of the diaconate shall be known as deacons and

147

deaconesses". But again this was slow to happen because individual men hesitated to be the first; they would feel more comfortable if there were a group. There was in fact a group of men trained and ready for the diaconate, who seemed to be the obvious first entrants and with whom the Deaconess Council had built up quite close relationships. These were the lay missionaries, agents of the Home Board appointed to parishes to preach and exercise pastoral care under the direction of a minister and Kirk Session. They were commissioned by a Court of the Church; many of them served as elders, but they had no council or corporate identity of their own.

The spheres of ministry of lay missionaries had developed over the years. Whereas in earlier years the great majority worked in Highland parishes where there was no resident minister and their service was therefore to do the work of a minister so far as that was possible without ordination, by 1988 only a minority were in such appointments. The majority were serving in parishes and other appointments, closely parallel to the appointments of deaconesses, in areas of need. There had also been a change in their training, which was now the same as that of deaconesses, namely the two-year course at St Colm's.

It has to be said that the Home Board and its successor, the Board of Ministry and Mission, who were very much in control of the lay missionaries, did not encourage the idea — even after 1979 — that they might become deacons, until a dramatic moment in the autumn of 1987. On the morning of September 18 I received a telephone call from Dr Ian Doyle, Secretary of the Mission Committee in the Board, asking if I could look in to see him. In his office he took me completely by surprise, saying he had always wanted the lay missionaries to amalgamate with the deaconesses in one diaconate, and that he thought our Centenary Year would be a good time for that to happen. When I suggested that he had kept his great desire a closely guarded secret, he agreed laughingly that perhaps this had been so. He told me that at a meeting of lay missionaries the previous day he had put to them the suggestion that they might "seek for amalgamation and unity under a diaconate, revised in whatever way might seem good to all concerned". This suggestion had been generally agreed among them, and they, with the Mission Committee, would now like to consult with the Diaconate Committee.

The deaconesses were overjoyed and could scarcely believe that the door on which we had been knocking for some time should now suddenly have been opened from the other side. A process of consultation began. It was established that there was no need to 'revise the diaconate', as had been suggested: that would have implied some inadequacy in the current scheme to encompass men. With the guidance of the Principal Clerk we reached the conclusion that what we should ask the Assembly to do, in accordance with decisions already taken in 1979, was to "declare that all lay missionaries are eligible to be recognised as holding the office of the diaconate, and authorise the Diaconate Committee to recognise as deacons all lay missionaries who may be recommended for this purpose by the Mission Committee of the Board of Ministry and Mission". This the General Assembly agreed to on May 23 1988.

Of the 19 lay missionaries currently serving, 17 applied to become deacons. These names were submitted to the office-bearers of the Diaconate Committee who had been given powers to recognise them as deacons. The public acknowledgement of this historic step took place at a special meeting of the Diaconate Council held in Glasgow on St Columba's Day, June 9. At a Communion Service held in Renfield St Stephen's Church, these seventeen were welcomed into the diaconate and given their badges of office. It was not long before the first man was commissioned as a deacon. On September 8, Graham Austin, a former agricultural storeman from the Borders, made history when he was commissioned by the Presbytery of Lothian at Easthouses, Dalkeith, where he was already serving. Others have followed, and there are now regularly men in training for the diaconate. We have at last reached the situation in which both women and men may serve in that ministry which is appropriate to their gifts and calling rather than to their sex.

* * * * *

It seemed to me good that the Diaconate Committee, as the agent of the General Assembly, should contribute to the centenary celebrations by mounting an event which might advance the whole Church's perception of the diaconate. This event should transcend the usual frontiers both between denominations and between the different ministries. The Committee took up the proposal, and in 1987 the Assembly approved it and authorised the Committee to issue invitations in the name of the Church of Scotland to a Scottish Ecumenical Encounter on the Diaconate (SEED) to be held in 1988. The aim would be, in the words of our Report, "to bring together representatives of those who serve as deacons and deaconesses in the Churches in Britain with those whose task it is to formulate doctrines of ministry and those who take decisions and make appointments".

The objective would be that in meeting together we might come to value and accept one another across the barriers which too often separate those exercising different roles; that we might share problems and dreams; that we might reach a deeper understanding of the diaconate and help each other to discuss the way forward.

The planning from the start was ecumenical; we invited other churches in Scotland — Episcopal, Roman Catholic, Methodist — to join with us on a planning committee. We intended to invite all churches in the British Isles who were known to have an interest in the diaconate, though it was quite difficult in this unexplored territory to find the appropriate authority in the other churches. We were nonetheless aware that in many branches of the Church there was a ferment of thought about the diaconate, and this gave us ground to hope that if we could locate the interested parties in the various denominations they might be as eager as we were to meet and share.

In the event SEED was a quite remarkable occasion. We met at Scottish Churches' House, Dunblane, from 26 to 30 September. Thirty-two people — deacons (women and men), trainers, theologians, administrators — represented the Roman Catholic Church in England and Wales and in Scotland, the Church of England, the Church in Wales, the Scottish Episcopal Church, the Methodist Church, the Presbyterian Church in Ireland and the Church of Scotland. In our own case, as well as deacons and deaconesses and some of the Committee, the Conveners of the Panel on Doctrine, the Ministry Committee and the Mission Committee, as well as the Principal Clerk, participated.

In spite of the wide variety of interpretation of the office of the diaconate, the participants at SEED seemed to find an immediate rapport with one another. This was possibly just because variety is of the essence of the diaconate, as are adaptability to need and response to new challenges. The people gathered at Dunblane were therefore not trammelled by theological definitions and ecclesiastical status-seeking; they were open to each other and willing to learn. There were many areas in which we did learn from one another. For example, we in the Church of Scotland may well have something to learn from the Roman Catholic and Anglican Churches, whose deacons have a clearly defined liturgical role, whereas ours do not. On the other hand, the Church of England, pioneering in one diocese the training of non-stipendiary permanent deacons, were very interested to know more about our specialised diaconal training at St Colm's.

SEED was described in *Distinctive Diaconate News* (a periodical newssheet edited by Sister Teresa, Deacon of the Community of St Andrew in London), as "a major occasion for the diaconate movement in the UK". The same *News* noted that "SEED was unique in the dialogue it began not only ecumenically, but also between those responsible for theology and administration of ministerial work within the various churches, and those practising the diaconate". So fruitful was the Encounter found to be that a second (SEED II) was held in September 1991, hosted by the Scottish Episcopal Church. This also expressed the same desire to move forward together, and it is hoped that the Roman Catholic Church will host SEED III in 1994.

In this way the Diaconate Committee of the Church of Scotland has been able to make a useful contribution to the ecumenical discussion on the diaconate. Another important strand in this discussion, interwoven with both SEED I and SEED II, has been the contribution of the Working Party on the Diaconate of the Multilateral Church Conversation in Scotland. Their Report, *Deacons for Scotland?*, (Saint Andrew Press, 1990) is a valuable document, to which I shall refer later.

* * * * *

We turn now to the question of membership of the Courts of the Church, an issue which had been before the Church for many years and was finally resolved in 1990. It would seem to be common sense that deacons and deaconesses as trained and commissioned servants of the Church, many with years of valuable experience, should have some part in the decision-making processes. But common sense is seldom allowed to decide an issue of this sort in the Church. There were a number of factors militating against such an innovation. First, that it would be an innovation, upsetting the four-hundred-year-old tradition of Courts composed exclusively of ministers and elders and the supposedly sacrosanct principle of a balance between these two in the superior Courts. But, of course, the Church is free, according to her own Declaratory Articles, to determine the constitution and membership of her own Courts. There was the fairly prevalent objection when this matter was raised that the deaconesses' role was a servant role, and they should not seek any kind of status for themselves. We had to reply that it was really not a matter of status, but of bringing to an end the exclusion of those who had a contribution to make.

After 1965, when women were declared to be eligible for the eldership, there was the further objection raised to our case, namely that deaconesses should be content to be elders and play their part in that capacity. But that served only to confuse the issue: deaconesses are not elders, and to have pretended that they were would have sold the pass. The Deaconess Council, though it had no power to coerce, advised deaconesses not to accept the eldership but to wait until the Church saw fit to accept them into membership by virtue of their own office. We were supported in this in 1968 by the General Administration Committee, who disagreed with a proposal from the Panel on Doctrine that deaconesses should become "a special class of elder".

Furthermore, the objection was raised: if deaconesses were to become members of Church Courts, what about the lay missionaries? There seemed to be a curious assumption that it would not be right to include in Church Courts those holding an office all of whom were women. A proposal put to the Assembly in 1974 that deaconesses should, by virtue of their own office, have membership in the Courts of the Church was rejected. There was no move to grant this even in 1979 when the Assembly declared the diaconate to be an office open to both men and women. The Church was not yet ready.

However, in the 1980s the scene began to change and the

thinking of the Church to mature. The accession of the lay missionaries to the diaconate in 1988 undoubtedly clarified the situation for many, especially for those who could not conceive of an office of ministry in which there were no men. And the mind of the Church clarified as to the distinctiveness of the office of the diaconate. For example, the Panel on Doctrine in their 1989 report on "The Ministries of the Church" distinguished the diaconate clearly from the eldership, and said, "The Panel believes that members of the diaconate should have a recognised place in the Courts of the Church. They should be able to attend as of right the Kirk Session of the congregation in which they serve. They should be members of Presbytery and be eligible for membership of the General Assembly. It is long overdue that those who exercise such an important ministry, and are trained to work with others, are allowed to contribute fully in making the decisions about the Church's life and mission".

In 1987, the Diaconate Committee was given an explicit remit by the Assembly to take up this issue yet again. It was not of our seeking: on a motion from the floor of the House, the Assembly agreed to "invite the Diaconate Committee to consult with the Board of Practice and Procedure as to the position of members of the diaconate in relation to the Courts of the Church, and to report to the General Assembly of 1988". As Convener, I accepted this gladly, and the Committee embarked on the required consultation.

In 1988 we were able to report progress. We had consulted with the Legal Questions Committee of the Board of Practice and Procedure, and there had been tri-partite discussions between representatives of that Board, the Panel on Doctrine and the Diaconate Committee. We found to our immense satisfaction that the experts found no reason constitutionally or in doctrine for excluding deacons and deaconesses from Church courts. They accepted our case that if it were possible, it should be done in order to give proper recognition to the office and for the contribution they could make. It was then a matter of preparing legislation to bring to the following Assembly. This we proceeded to do with the advice of the Principal Clerk, James Weatherhead.

In 1989 I presented the Committee's Report, in which we set out the draft legislation proposed, together with the argument to support it. We argued that it would be both possible and right for the Assembly to take this step. It was constitutionally possible for the supreme Court to change the composition of the Courts. The Principal Clerk had given it as his opinion that the basis on which membership of Church Courts had hitherto been restricted to ministers and elders was that they had made a commitment to the Church's doctrinal standards and to its discipline. Deacons and deaconesses also fulfilled that condition. We reported also that there had been found to be no doctrinal reason to exclude the diaconate.

Moreover, there was clear agreement among the consulting parties that it would be right and to the advantage of the Church to include the diaconate in the Courts where their insights and experience could be heard. Because they were neither ministers nor elders it was necessary to make legislative provision for this third constituent group in the Courts.

The legislation proposed was the amendment of an Act of Assembly which defined Membership of Presbyteries. It was a somewhat complicated operation, but the gist was that the diaconate should be full members of Presbytery (not corresponding members as hitherto), attend Kirk Session as of right (not only by invitation) and be eligible for commissions to the General Assembly (i.e. to take their turn to be elected by Presbyteries to be members of the Assembly). This was accepted by the General Assembly who then, because it was legislation affecting the constitution of the Church, had to refer it to Presbyteries for the vote for or against; and if there were a majority in favour the Assembly would be able to pass it into law the following year. This is the Barrier Act procedure.

In the course of the ensuing winter Presbyteries gave their approval to this measure by a majority of 36 to 12. It therefore came back to the Assembly of 1990, which was free to convert the measure into a Standing Law of the Church or not, as they saw fit. There was an Order of the Day for this item of business at 7pm on Monday May 21 and quite a number of the diaconate were present in the galleries to witness what they hoped would be the last occasion on which they would be excluded from membership.

A curious anomaly in the Assembly's procedures worked to our advantage. The Assembly had finished its business unexpectedly by lunch-time and could not proceed to the rest of its day's programme because of the Order of the Day. This meant that the commissioners had a free afternoon, which James Weatherhead put to good use in preparing a speech to make when, as Principal Clerk, he presented to the Assembly the result of the Presbyteries' vote. Instead of the usual formal presentation of his report, he gave a masterly address answering the negative points made by those who had voted against, and setting out the argument for the Church taking this new step. Speaking with humour and conviction, he clearly had the Assembly with him as he gave it as his opinion that there was little substance in the objections which had been raised and went on to look at the positive advantages which would accrue to the Church, reaching the conclusion that "what is now proposed is good and right and much to be desired". He reminded the Assembly that membership of Church Courts involved not only government but also "the exercise of God's gifts of grace and love in directing and supervising the worship and mission and pastoral care of the Church". In this the diaconate were well qualified to share.

We could not have hoped for a more eloquent and authoritative advocacy. I sat in the Assembly with all my arguments marshalled, expecting to have to defend the proposal against the old objections. But these all withered away: no opposition was expressed, and the Assembly voted in favour. It was now the law of the Church that deacons and deaconesses employed within the Church or in certain specified appointments outside the Church were members of Presbytery by virtue of the office they held. This was what we had been struggling for for years, and among the diaconate there was a great sense of rejoicing at having at last achieved it. It was another historic moment, comparable in my view to the 1968 Act admitting women to the ordained ministry.

In my letter to the diaconate that summer I suggested that this marked not so much the end of all our striving as the beginning of new opportunities. Perhaps now the common gender term 'deacon' should be adopted by all: perhaps in the long-term the role of the Diaconate Council should be re-assessed; more immediately it became possible to produce a satisfactory revision of the Service of Commissioning. I was at this point handing over the convenership, but was asked to carry through to its completion our work on the Commissioning Service.

*　*　*　*　*

Since 1949, when Deaconesses and Church Sisters were amalgamated, all who held this office had been 'commissioned' by the appropriate Presbytery. In 1958 the Assembly authorised a Form of Service for the Commissioning of a Deaconess, which was published in the 1962 Ordinal and was still in use in 1986 when I became Convener, but was generally thought to be in need of revision. We worked on this for five years, finally producing a form of Service which was authorised by the Assembly in 1991.

There were a number of principles at stake. First, should the authorisation given to a deacon or deaconess by a

Presbytery be an act of 'commissioning' or of 'ordination'? There were some among the deaconesses who were anxious that the Church should use the term 'ordination', as she does not only for the ministry but also for the eldership. But some of us, including myself, have maintained that ordination belongs properly to the Ministry of Word and Sacraments (*pace* the eldership), and that to avoid confusion we should be better to keep the conception of commissioning, which is a good word conveying an appropriate meaning. If then we keep commissioning, do we nevertheless base the service as closely as possible on the Ordination Service, adapting it where necessary; or do we do our own thing and frame a service which is a genuine diaconate service, deriving elements from other diaconal traditions rather than from the ordination tradition? Our first revision took the latter course, but the subsequent and final version swung back more closely to the Service of Ordination. This was partly because a new Ordination Service was published in the meantime, which the diaconate found to be more congenial. Another question was the use of contemporary and inclusive language, and this the new Ordination Service provided. One other point was that, even though the Commissioning is an act of the Presbytery, we were keen that there should be adequate participation both by the diaconate and by the congregation. This has, I think, been achieved.

Curiously enough, however, the thorniest question of all proved to be that of the laying on of hands. We had been told firmly that the laying on of hands by the Presbytery belongs in the Ordination Service and there only. We therefore did not include this in our first revision but instead suggested a rather awkward substitute of 'taking hands' as a sign of welcome. But the Diaconate Council themselves insisted that nothing less than the laying of the hands of members of Presbytery on the head of the candidate during the prayer of commissioning would satisfy them. We therefore had to try again to formulate an acceptable rite of commissioning by prayer and the laying on of hands. I wrote a short paper asking the question, Why should not the Church *commission* by prayer and the laying on of hands?, and giving reasons from the New Testament and the practice of the Church to suggest that this might well be possible without causing any confusion with ordination.

We then sought the opinion of the Panel on Doctrine who said that in their view commissioning by prayer and the laying on of hands should be perfectly acceptable as an act of the Presbytery, provided that it was the Presbytery who were laying on hands. The question then arose, which members of Presbytery should lay hands? In Ordination it is the ministerial members who do this; therefore in Commissioning it should be the diaconal members. In the Panel's view the appropriate action was that in the prayer of commissioning the Moderator and the diaconate members of Presbytery should gather round and lay hands on the head of the candidate. The main body of ministers and elders would not be visibly involved, and there would be no danger of confusion in the mind of the Church as to what was happening.

That seemed to cut the Gordian knot at a stroke, and was absolutely splendid — provided that there were any such beings as diaconate members of the Presbytery. It would, of course, all depend on whether the General Assembly passed the necessary legislation the following year. As we have seen, they did; so after the Assembly of 1990 we were able to finalise a Form of Service for the Commissioning of a Deacon or Deaconess, which incorporates the act of commissioning by prayer and the laying on of hands. The Service has been well received and it remains to be seen whether it will stand the test of use.

In 1987 I was invited by the Friends of St Colm's to give the annual St Colm's Lecture. St Colm's was celebrating another centenary — that of the *training* of deaconesses, begun at

'The Institution' at 33 Mayfield Gardens, Edinburgh on November 16 1887. This seemed an appropriate occasion to speak about the diaconate, and I took for my theme the question "Does the Church need a diaconate?". (*St Colm's Education Centre and College*)

The implication in the title of this lecture was that there is a case to be argued, and I still (1992) think this is so. There is a certain elusiveness about the diaconate: it is hard to define and pin down: literature on the subject is full of expressions such as "the true diaconate" (Calvin), "the real diaconate", "authentic diaconate", "distinctive diaconate" used to distinguish what the writer believes to be the genuine or biblical concept in distinction from various aberrations. Calvin observed that in the Roman Church of his day "the legitimate order of deacons" has long ago been abolished, "having become only a step to the priesthood"; and concluded "The order of the diaconate should be restored to its integrity". Today, Roman and Anglican Churches speak of the 'transitional diaconate' when they mean a step to the priesthood; and we have used the term deacon (though now less commonly) to refer to those who administer congregational finances in Deacons' Courts. The terms deacon and diaconate therefore have to be rescued from what I believe to be misuse.

There is a case to be argued for a number of reasons. There is a general assumption that the normal pattern of congregational life is a congregation led by one professional minister who does everything: that may be an acceptable pattern in some places, but is inadequate in many others. Secondly, Presbyterianism, for many Scots the bedrock of their churchmanship, is perceived as leadership and government by ministers and elders: the impact of the small number of the diaconate now incorporated into the system is bound to be little noticed for some time. The diaconate is only known in certain areas of the Church's life and of the country, and where it is known there is still the perception that this is a women's ministry. The case has also to be argued in the light of a renewed and very welcome emphasis on the ministry of the whole laity: fear may be expressed that the diaconate is attempting to usurp functions which belong to all the people. It has to be shown then that a deacon is fully lay; he or she makes no claim to any exclusive function. But there are congregations where the need is for a trained, articulate, professional person to act as a catalyst to enable the diakonia of the whole.

The Church has yet to take fully into her thinking the fact that ministers, deacons and elders all share in leadership. More important, she has yet to give full weight to the fact that there are now alternative avenues of service for both men and women; that the diaconate is not inferior but different. (At SEED II an American Lutheran deacon expressed his astonishment that in our system, although people may move from the diaconate to the ministry, no one would think of moving the other way because the pay is less.)

In my lecture, having given a brief historical and ecumenical overview, I answered my own question in the affirmative. I believe it is important that there should be a different kind of professional ministry in the Church, complementary to that of Word and Sacraments.

From the starting-point of the needs of today's society — needs arising from widespread spiritual and material deprivation — it seems clear that the Church, having lost so much ground, now has to mobilise all her resources if she is to provide what people are looking for. She cannot do this by relying solely on ministers with an academic training and a commission to provide the ordinances of religion. We need to deploy also people skilled in youth work, group work, community work; those who can be where people are, encouraging and enabling; people with gifts and training and freedoms different from those of the ordained ministry.

From the point of view of the health of the Church, we

161

have for too long had a monolithic ministry, and we are suffering the consequences in a 'leader and led' mentality. Ministers have had to be one-man-bands, and have taken on functions which could be better allocated to others. Differentiation of function, giving scope to specialised skills, is bound to be healthy and effective. The New Testament Church learned this very early on: whether or not the Seven appointed to 'serve tables' in Acts 6 can technically be called deacons, what is beyond dispute is that here is a differentiation of function among Church officials — even if Stephen immediately oversteps the boundaries and proceeds to preach. The New Testament Church exhibits, in fact, a wide variety of ministries responding to the wide variety of gifts which are freely given by the Spirit to the People of God. We need to rediscover some of these gifts and make use of them.

My main plea would be that the Church should rediscover her own freedom. So much of the time we seem to be bound by our history and tradition, and we imagine that we have to follow what has always been. It should not be like that: tradition and law should be for our protection and guidance, not for our chains. We have been set free by the gospel; the Church can do new things in response to new situations. Why is there such resistance to change? Why should it be necessary to wrestle long and hard in order to effect the most obvious and commonsense innovations?

In his Baird Lectures (*The Church of Christ: its Life and Work*, Macmillan, 1905) Professor Charteris maintained, with regard to forms of ministry, that "the Church is free from the bondage of any letter in regard to her officials. The spirit of Christ which is in her is free to choose a mode of working adapted to the special needs of changing times". For him this meant, among many other innovations the restoration of the diaconate. For us, a century later, it means still trying to catch up with his vision and going on from there.

The diaconate itself exhibits a kind of freedom, akin to the elusiveness we noted earlier, which may be difficult for the Church to come to terms with, but which none the less should be very useful to her. Dr Charteris himself noted that in the early centuries of the Church deaconesses were eventually superseded by nuns, who were easier for the male ecclesiastical authorities to manage. "The diaconate was too free an order — of too miscellaneous usefulness — to be under the dominion of men," says Charteris, "and so it disappeared". Today deacons and deaconesses should be seen to have a certain freedom, not available to fully stretched ministers, a freedom to move out in new ways, out into society. It is to be hoped that the Church will not find them too difficult to manage, but will give them all the encouragement and support she can muster.

Let the last word be an ecumenical one. The Report *Deacons for Scotland?*, published by the Multilateral Church Conversation and already referred to above, is chiefly concerned to make the point that the six churches engaged in this Conversation should not seek to reach an agreed definition of the office of deacon prior to union, but should agree to take a variety of kinds of deacon into a united Church. Variety and adaptability characterise the diaconate, so that differences between the churches are a ground of hope rather than a problem. Furthermore, the Report suggests that the story of the diaconate which we have been tracing in these pages may have a contribution to make. I quote, "All the more significant is the development of a new kind of diaconate in the Church of Scotland, generally but not necessarily full-time, characterised as was the Patristic Diaconate by the great variety of work being undertaken by different Deacons, including pastoral work and teaching. The continuing evolution of this office, and the Church's continuing quest for a theology of it in relation to other ministries of the Church, are full of promise for the future of Scottish Christianity" (op cit pp 62-63).

X — Queen's Chaplain

If the case for the diaconate has still to be argued it is not in the Courts of the Church: the General Assembly has pronounced again and again that this scriptural office is valid and to be valued. But in the hearts and minds of people — even in high places — the diaconate has yet to be fully acknowledged. It is hard to understand why this should be so, when deacons and deaconesses are such a selfless gift to the Church. And yet it is so: and there is still work to be done in gaining full acceptance for them, in improving their living and working conditions and in clarifying their administrative structures.

Similarly, with regard to the ordination of women, the General Assembly has pronounced that all offices in the Church are now open to women as to men. Yet, not all hearts and minds are won. There are still doubts in some quarters even about women in the eldership, and the Assembly of 1991 had to make it clear yet again that it is against the law of the Church to exclude anyone from that office on grounds of sex.

The land is not yet fully possessed. Perhaps this is because the numbers both of the diaconate and of women in the ordained ministry represent very small minorities within the whole. There are currently only seventy deacons and deaconesses in comparison with over one thousand ministers. Of those thousand, only about 15% are women. In these circumstances the significance of the contributions made both by the diaconate and by ordained women may well be overlooked. There is still discrimination against women in the Church, hidden and unacknowledged for the most part. Our freedom in the gospel is not yet fully realised.

The situation in 1992, however, is very different from that of 1952 when I was a deaconess candidate. We have come a long way in these forty years, and I find myself looking back with considerable satisfaction on what has been achieved. I am aware of a degree of acceptance possible now which was not possible then, and I am immensely grateful to so many people who have helped to bring this about by their vision and courage, sympathy and support, and — perhaps most of all — by allowing their minds to be changed by the argument and having the courage to say so.

A woman who is a minister is still a strange phenomenon in the eyes of many in society at large. A woman who is a minister and is the recipient of an honour or is appointed to high office is still enough of a rarity to excite a quite disproportionate amount of interest in the media. No woman has yet been elected to the highest office in the Church of Scotland, the Moderatorship of the General Assembly, an office confined to ministers and held for one year.

Since my retirement in 1983 people have frequently said to me: "We hope you will be Moderator of the General Assembly". My inner response to that has been that, for me, that would be quite unthinkable: I should by no means be suitable or capable for that supreme office, and to be the first woman so selected would be unimaginably daunting. However, as a woman in a man's world, one is under great pressure not to decline any office lest it be said that women are not willing to shoulder the top responsibilities. It may be that, in a given situation, one is the only woman available for a particular appointment and if one declines, then the appointment goes to a man again, and we women cannot complain: we have been given the chance and passed it up. The burden of being willing to consider 'impossible' tasks can be heavy, and one finds oneself frequently in situations which in prospect were inconceivable. In the case of the Moderatorship, I had to think the unthinkable and make up my mind to allow my name to be proposed.

The Moderator is elected by the Assembly on the

nomination of a Committee whose deliberations are naturally entirely confidential. All I can say is that I was asked more than once to let my name go forward, but I was not nominated.

At that time there was something of an anti-feminist backlash in the Church which, according to one leading churchman, set back "the cause of women" by twenty years. He was referring to the so-called Motherhood of God debate, of which I should give a brief account.

In the General Assembly of 1984 there was a painful fiasco, when the Assembly refused even to discuss the report of a study which the Woman's Guild and the Panel on Doctrine had undertaken at the invitation of the Assembly of 1982. At the Annual Meeting of the Guild in April of that year, the President, Mrs Anne Hepburn, had used a prayer which addressed God not only as "Our Father" but also as "God our Mother" and "Dear Mother God". There was intense reaction to this; the matter was raised in the Assembly, and it was agreed that the concept of the motherhood of God merited biblical and theological study. It was therefore extremely distressing when two years later the Assembly refused even to receive the careful biblical study which they were offered. The Church was evidently not yet ready to talk about the use of feminine symbolism to represent the deity.

I had no part in this controversy, and I am not sure whether its effect on the Church has been beneficial or the reverse. In the long-term it was right that the Assembly should be faced with the issues of feminine symbolism and language, but it has also to be said that in the short-term 'women's issues' were curiously lumped together in the minds of many in the Church, with the result that emotional reaction to the debate spilled over into a kind of anti-woman feeling — the feeling that women could not be trusted with theology and worship. The wrestling was evidently not yet finished.

The Presbytery of Edinburgh invited me to be their Moderator for 1988. I had thought I was quite safe from that honour ever coming my way. It normally falls to one of the more senior ministers in that large and august body, and senior I certainly was not, having been ordained for only ten years. However, for reasons best known to themselves, the nominating Committee decided to depart from usual practice and to approach me. Again, I was reluctant; but again, I felt the pressure of the expectations of others that I should accept, and this I did.

My reluctance was partly due to the face that I, together I think with most other women members, find the Presbytery a very intimidating body because of its size (well over 400 members) and formality; and, it has to be said, because of its male dominance. These difficulties become greater rather than smaller when viewed from the Moderator's chair, and I never really felt at ease in meetings. The problem was exacerbated by the knowledge that the spotlight was on me as the first woman to hold that office. Press interest was considerable and, to an extent, out of all proportion to the magnitude of the appointment: after all, some fifty men ministers are appointed every year as moderators of presbyteries, and no one pays much heed. What's special about a woman's appointment? A further factor is that a woman in that situation is aware that her performance will be assessed, favourably or otherwise, and with it the putative performance of *all* women. On the other hand, there was encouragement from remarks made by other women to the effect that they felt affirmed by seeing "one of us up there".

Apart from presiding over the business at monthly meetings, there are other aspects to the task of a Presbytery Moderator. The liturgical functions include presiding not only at Communion and other worship in the Presbytery, but also at services of ordination and induction and of commissioning to the diaconate — all in parish churches where, it might be said, the real life of the Church is to be found. This is an enormous privilege for any minister, and one that I found very rewarding and uplifting; to have a share in this way in the great succession of the Church and her ministry is an awesome experience on which I shall always look back with great pride.

There is also the representative function. For one year one finds oneself representing that part of the national church which is within and around the city of Edinburgh, the seat of a Roman Catholic archdiocese and an Episcopal diocese. I found nothing but warm acceptance from the Archbishop and Bishop, who might have been expected to have difficulties with the colleagueship of a woman, and I enjoyed working with them in, for example, setting up the new Edinburgh Churches' Council (now "Edinburgh Churches Together"). There is no doubt, however, that our system of an annual change of moderator puts him or her at a disadvantage in inter-church relations: there is not nearly enough time to develop fruitful relationships. The Moderator of Presbytery is also honoured by various invitations to services and other functions in the city. I did my best to represent the Church on all such occasions, and I made a point of reporting monthly to the Presbytery on what I had been doing on their behalf.

By a curious accident of history the District Council of Edinburgh elected a woman for the first time as Lord Provost in the same year that the Presbytery had, for the first time, a woman as Moderator. I had the great pleasure of calling on Mrs Eleanor McLaughlin in the City Chambers, as was the custom, and of welcoming her to a meeting of Presbytery when she was invited to address us. It was good to find another woman in a comparable appointment.

Since the main theme of this book is the acceptance of women in ministry in the Church, I should say that so far as I was aware my moderatorship of the Presbytery was acceptable to the Church in Edinburgh. There may well have been those in the Presbytery, including some who were ordained or inducted in my year of office, who had difficulty with the idea of a woman in the moderator's chair. If so, nothing was said to me, and I was consistently treated with the respect and courtesy due to the office.

There was one sticky moment, which I record as an instance of the fact that we have not yet quite arrived at a natural and relaxed acceptance of one another. Just before my installation my predecessor in office, who was a bachelor, said that it would not be possible for him to be seen placing the moderator's ring on a woman's finger. Oh dear! had we really not grown beyond that yet? It has to be said that this ring had not been worn by my immediate predecessor nor his predecessors for ten years, but this was *not* the reason given for not putting it on my finger. I did wear it on official occasions, as have my successors; but I was always sorry that it had not been passed on to me formally in the succession. It is a symbol of the *episcope* exercised corporately by the Presbytery, of which the Moderator is *primus* (or in my case *prima*) *inter pares*, that is 'first among equals'.

I suppose that in all the varied tasks of my chequered career in the Church I have always hoped that through my ministry there might rub off something of the sense of the One Holy Catholic and Apostolic Church with which I had been imbued in my younger years and of which I have always been so vividly aware. How gratifying then that, at the end of my year as Moderator of Presbytery, one of my colleagues should have written to me: "You have constantly allowed us to breathe the atmosphere of the whole Church worldwide, and also of the continuing and Apostolic Church with all the strengths of our traditions. At the same time, we have clearly been the Church of this day and this place". Perhaps, after all, it has been worth sticking in and not allowing oneself to be deflected or letting the vision be diminished.

In Edinburgh the custom is that the one Presbytery

occasion on which the Moderator preaches is the Service for the Licensing of Students. In 1988 there were nine candidates for the ministry under the supervision of the Presbytery who had completed their studies and were to be licensed as preachers and made probationers for the holy ministry. St Andrew's and St George's Church was therefore full with all their friends and supporters, and it was a marvellous opportunity to say some of the things I believe about the task of preaching which the Church was laying upon these young people. For the calling of the preacher is of prime importance even in these days of questioning, discussion and participation. Preaching is the main opportunity the minister has to lead the people deeper in to the mystery of God and to explicate for them and with them the bearing of this mystery on their living and on the life of the world.

There is a paradox at the heart of preaching. The preacher has to proclaim the certainties of the faith and at the same time to go on exploring into the mysteries of God. Both of these are important, and both are lifelong tasks. How is preaching to reflect and respond to the holiness of God and also His love manifested in Jesus; to the glory of the invisible God and also His grace freely offered; to the mystery of the godhead and also the great certainties of the faith?

There are two conflicting temptations to which the preacher is prey. On one hand, some ministers disclaim any theological expertise with the lamentable remark "Of course, I am no theologian". They rely simply on a neat package of creeds and standards, watertight solutions for all problems, precise rules for living; a simplistic presentation which would fail to satisfy the intelligent theological curiosity of very many listeners. In honesty, even a professional Christian does not know all the answers: he or she will be better advised to admit to being an explorer together with his or her people. On the other hand there are those for whom all questions appear to be open: such preachers become so enmeshed in the tangles of enquiry and debate that they are left with nothing to proclaim, and the hungry sheep look up and are not fed.

The paradox is that the preacher has to be both a proclaimer and a pilgrim; the more one is the latter, the more effective will one be as the former, and *vice versa*. The more one explores into the mystery of God — in worship, in biblical study, in theological reading and discussion — the firmer one's grip is likely to become on the central truth of the gospel, which is the Cross and Resurrection, the victory of self-giving love. And, as I noted in Chapter 1, the more sure one is of the centre, the more free one is to be open-minded on much else.

My final word to these nine budding preachers was: "There is one message only to be proclaimed — the gospel of the grace of the Lord Jesus Christ. Beyond that, go on all your life long exploring the mystery of the God who is infinite and holy and glorious".

* * * * *

In 1991 a lovely and totally unexpected honour came my way: I was appointed by the Queen to be one of Her Majesty's Chaplains in Scotland. There are ten members of Her Majesty's Ecclesiastical Household in Scotland, and when one of these retires at the age of 70 a new appointment is made. The duties are not onerous: one can expect to be invited to preach at Crathie Kirk, which means an invitation to stay for two nights at Balmoral Castle as a guest of the Queen — a memorable experience. Apart from that, it is really very much an honour. In my case it was given rather later in life than normal, and it was all the more welcome for that. After many years of knocking on doors and sometimes pleading for acceptance for myself or my colleagues, it was marvellous that this honour should simply be bestowed *sola gratia*.

Nor was it, I was encouraged to believe, the appointment of a token woman. The Very Rev Robin Barbour, who was Dean of the Chapel Royal and therefore responsible for putting names forward to the Queen, was good enough to say in response to a press enquiry "There is no way she is a 'token woman'; she has been appointed because she is a person of real distinction . . . She championed the cause of women's ordination with great skill, devotion and sincerity without ever becoming shrill or difficult".

My appointment was the subject of speculation in a column in *The Glasgow Herald* on April 20, nearly a month before it was to be announced by Buckingham Palace. After an uncomfortable couple of weeks of stalling and "No comment", the news was broken by *The Times* with several column inches and a picture on the front page on May 8, still before the official announcement, which was due on May 14. The Palace now confirmed it, and the balloon was up. Radio and television expressed intense interest and I did a whole series of interviews that day, as well as profiles which appeared in the press on subsequent days.

Again, the interest focussed almost entirely on my being a woman. There were several attempts to draw me out on the relevance of my appointment to the argument currently raging in the Church of England about the ordination of women to the priesthood. In response I could only say that I did not think my appointment said anything about the Queen's views on that question: it meant only that she recognised the practice of the national Church in Scotland, which had been ordaining women to the ministry for the last twenty-three years.

I found a warm welcome from the other chaplains, and I had a considerable mailbag of congratulations and good wishes from a wide circle of friends. The service of induction in St Giles' Cathedral on the evening of Sunday June 23 was for me a most memorable occasion. The new Dean of the Chapel Royal, Dr William Morris of Glasgow

Cathedral, in inducting me, spoke personally and with great warmth. The large congregation — mainly friends from all the varied stages of my career right back to Musselburgh days — responded heartily to the minister's invitation to give me a round of applause.

What I found really heart-warming about this whole event was that it confirmed that all the wrestling that had gone on in years past had not stirred up lasting animosity or ill will. On the contrary, there appeared to be an immense reservoir of good will and gratitude for what had been achieved.

Deo gratia!

THE STRANGENESS OF GOD
by
Elizabeth Templeton

Essays in Contemporary Theology

A DAY AT
A TIME
by
Denis Duncan

A thought and a prayer for each day
of a year

ARTHUR JAMES
One Cranbourne Road, London N10 2BT

THROUGH PETER'S EYES
by Hazel Morgan

The world and its people as seen through the eyes of a boy with Down's Syndrome. Hazel Morgan pleads for changed attitudes to people with a handicap.

"I hope this book will be widely read for both its insights and its questions"
Bill Anderson in *The Methodist Recorder*

ISBN 85305 305 7

DEAR STEPHEN
by Anne Downey

A grieving mother's letter-diary of the year which followed her teenage son's suicide.

ISBN 85305 281 6

LOSS — AN INVITATION TO GROW
by Jean Grigor

A book on bereavement for the bereaved and those who minister to the bereaved.

ISBN 85305 269 7

SHEILA — A Healing through Dying
by Saxon Walker

A husband's tribute to his wife's courage and faith as she approached her death.

ISBN 85305 290 5

ARTHUR JAMES
One Cranbourne Road, London N10 2BT